EDUCATING THE INTELLIGENT

MICHAEL HUTCHINSON AND
CHRISTOPHER YOUNG

With three tables and nine diagrams

PENGUIN BOOKS

Penguin Books Ltd, Harmondsworth, Middlesex
U.S.A.: Penguin Books Inc., 3300 Clipper Mill Road, Baltimore 11, Md
AUSTRALIA: Penguin Books Pty Ltd, 762 Whitehorse Road,
Mitcham, Victoria

—

First published 1962
Reprinted 1964

—

—

Made and printed in Great Britain
by Hazell Watson & Viney Ltd
Aylesbury, Bucks
Set in Linotype Times

PELICAN BOOKS

A 566

EDUCATING THE INTELLIGENT

MICHAEL HUTCHINSON AND

CHRISTOPHER YOUNG

Michael Hutchinson was born in Lancashire in 1925 and educated at Marlborough College and Trinity Hall, Cambridge. He has been a schoolmaster for several years, teaching at St Columba's College, Dublin, and the City of London School. In 1956–7 he was a visiting lecturer in history at Middlebury College, Vermont, U.S.A. Recently he has administered the General Publications Section of the Ministry of Education in the Western Region of Nigeria. Widely travelled, he has contributed many articles to educational journals.

Christopher Young, who was born in 1929, was educated at Bryanston and King's College, London, where he read mathematics. After three years as an Instructor Officer in the Navy and five years at the City of London School, he is now teaching at King's College School, Wimbledon. In 1959 he took a degree in Economics, and he is a Fellow of the Royal Statistical Society. Christopher Young, who is married and has four children, formerly played Rugby for the Navy, captained the Hampshire team, and had a trial for Wales.

TO AUDREY

CONTENTS

LIST OF TABLES AND DIAGRAMS

ACKNOWLEDGEMENTS

WE wish to thank all those whose ideas have influenced our thought and whose expertise has provided us with the necessary background to write this book. In particular we acknowledge our indebtedness to the following:

All those whose published work is referred to in the text;

The correspondents who answered our questionnaires so fully;

Mr J. M. C. Davidson, Mr R. C. Holloway, Mr M. S. Justins, Mr W. D. H. Moore, Mr F. W. Ockenden, Mrs Ann Pennell, Dr W. L. Presswood, Mr M. S. Smith, Mr B. J. Stokes, Mr John Wakelin, Mr J. H. Wheeler, and Mr P. J. S. Whitmore for contributing papers on special topics;

Mr B. L. Adams, Mr Michael Powell, Mr Stirrat Johnson Marshall, and Mr Peter Smithson for giving us the benefit of their experience in school architecture;

Dr J. G. P. Hunt and Mr W. A. Wessell for helping us to draw up the diagram of 'Comparison of Average Salaries';

Mr Peter Jones for making the diagrams of our 'Plan for the Secondary School';

Mr G. H. Clark for reading the text and making suggestions for its greater clarity.

Our special debt to Mr Bryan Spielman who persuaded us to draw up a list of needs of the child and to Mr A. D. C. Peterson for the stimulus of the 1960–1 Oxford Conferences on Sixth-Form Education.

Lastly, in thanking all these and other personal friends for their help and encouragement, we must absolve them from the responsibility for the opinions expressed in the text, and any errors of fact must be attributed to our own carelessness.

INTRODUCTION

THIS is a book for parents, teachers, and all who are interested in education. We have attempted to answer the exciting questions – 'How do we want our children to be brought up?' 'What sort of life should they be prepared to live?' 'What should they be taught at school?' It is a book about the kind of secondary education that we ought to be providing for our more intelligent children. What we have to say applies to no more than the top forty per cent of the intelligence range of our children. The curriculum which we construct in answer to these and other questions will not be suitable for all secondary schools. This is not because the rest are unimportant – far from it – and indeed there is another book waiting to be written about the secondary curriculum for the other sixty per cent of our children. However, we are not the people to write it. In this book we have written from our own experience.

The reason for writing the book is that we believe that in many ways the secondary education at present offered to our more intelligent children is out of date. Much of it is on the right lines, but has been overtaken by the rapid changes both in the intellectual world and in our society during the first half of this century, and some of it is plainly obsolete. We have therefore begun by asking some key questions about the needs of the child and the needs of the society to which the child will belong. These questions, which we discuss in Chapter 2, provide the framework within which we construct the curriculum of Chapters 4 and 5. What should emerge is a new concept of secondary education which is not only up to date but also sufficiently flexible to meet some of our future requirements in education.

Working from first principles, using only ethics and our existent civilization as a guide, is exciting. But it has been even more exciting because we have tried at every stage to produce a concept of secondary education that is severely practical. Our initial test of new ideas, or the modification of old ideas, has been – *Will they work?* In the latter part of the book, in dealing with some of the technical problems which loom large in education – examinations, for example – we offer practical solutions for gearing them to the curriculum that we have built up. We ask no better than to be judged by the test of practicality and we shall be satisfied if some of our readers find themselves saying: 'But why haven't we done this before?'

The book was finished in August 1961. Since then there have been important developments in many of the fields which we discuss: an increased awareness of the need for better state education, shown by the formation of the new Associations for the Advancement of State Education; the acceptance by the teachers of a salary award of £42m., the largest ever increase in the history of their negotiations; the setting up of a Curriculum Study Group by the Ministry of Education; new proposals by the Vice-Chancellors' committee for university entrance requirements; the publication of *Investment for National Survival*, written by a committee described as 'one of the most high-powered ever to have considered educational topics'; and increased interest in education shown by newspapers, periodicals, radio, television, and political parties. Our figures, we feel, are not invalidated by these events, because in every case we have used them to illustrate more general arguments – this is particularly true in our discussion of teachers' salaries – and nothing that has happened since the book was written would make us want to change any of these arguments.

For the rest of this century we shall increasingly depend upon today's intelligent children – our rulers of tomorrow. Of course the right education won't solve all their problems. But it lies within our power to prepare them for the future rather than for the past. This, surely, is the concern of us all.

London M.E.H.
June 1962 C.D.Y.

CHAPTER 1

Investment in Education

RECENTLY our government spent £100 million on the development of a weapon, the Blue Streak rocket missile, which is apparently useless. Luckily we are still a very rich nation and we appear to be able to lose this large sum of money and remain solvent. The long-suffering British taxpayer, through his representatives in Parliament, expressed his disapproval, tightened his belt one more notch, and paid the bill. The money had been lost, but thanks to the development of American weapons no further serious damage appeared to have been caused. The government would be able to buy or build another weapon which would meet the need for which Blue Streak was originally intended. It was just a question of starting again.

Unfortunately there is no such easy let-out when we consider the question of investment in education. If a child is illiterate when he leaves school we cannot start again; he will remain illiterate for the rest of his life. If a child is innumerate* when he leaves school we cannot start again; he will remain innumerate for the rest of his life. If a child is amoral when he leaves school we cannot start again; he will remain amoral for the rest of his life. If the amount of investment in education is inadequate to fulfil the purposes of education we cannot redress this inadequacy. We have on our hands a generation of under-educated men and women. And they will be on our hands for ten, twenty, thirty, forty, even fifty years. There is absolutely nothing we can do about it.

But if our investment in education is adequate to fulfil the purposes of education we get a long-term return on our money

* The antithesis of numerate. Numeracy has been defined as 'an understanding of the basic nature and aims of science' (Science Masters' Association: *Science and Education*, 1961).

that is second to no other investment. For we are investing in the lives of men and women. We are investing in their productive capacity. We are investing in the homes and families that they will build. We are investing in the contribution that they will make to the culture of the nation. We are investing in the ideas and beliefs of our civilization. The money we spend on weapons will ensure our physical survival, but the money we spend on education will determine the kind of society in which we shall survive. We get the return on our weapon investment now, but we shall get the return on our education investment over the next ten, twenty, thirty, forty, or fifty years. Are we investing enough to ensure that we will get this return?

One measure of public education expenditure is to take it as a percentage of the net national income:

1937–8	2·5 per cent
1947–8	2·7 per cent
1954–5	3·3 per cent
1957–8	4·3 per cent

At the current rate of expenditure

we are ahead (at the moment) of the Common Market (except France); but substantially behind the United States (over 5 per cent) and the Soviet Union (probably between 6 per cent and 7 per cent.(71)*

Despite the fact that expenditure on education almost doubled between 1948 and 1958, Britain's rate of growth in educational expenditure will have to be increased if it is to match Continental rates of growth.

Federal Germany will probably double its expenditure between 1960 and 1970. By 1970 Federal Germany will have 300,000 university students with a similar total population to that of Britain; France will have 500,000; the United Kingdom will have 170,000. . . . Britain shows distinct signs of lagging behind after a decade of considerable advance.(71)

In the expansion of an educational system it is necessary not only to expand the total amount of money invested but also to

* These figures relate to the References, page 233 ff.

invest the money in the right sectors at the right time. For example, it is no use building splendid new schools if there are not enough teachers to use them efficiently. Similarly, it is no use providing more places in colleges of technology if there are no facilities for teaching science at school to would-be technologists. Now one of the weighty reasons given for the fact that Britain has fewer university places in proportion to her population than almost every other advanced country is simply that she has got fewer boys and girls ready to take advantage of them. This poses the question of whether the education they receive in secondary schools is anything like as efficient as it should be.

Is investment in primary and secondary education being carried out with the maximum *educational* efficiency? As late as 1955 it was not, for

> if 'social' expenditure, like school meals, milk, and the health service, is excluded from the calculation [of expenditure], then expenditure in 1955 was a lower proportion of the national income than in the pre-war years from 1931 to 1935.(72)

And on the same question the Crowther Report states that

> it appears to be demonstrable that the total cost of education in schools in 1955, expressed as a proportion of the total real national income, did not substantially exceed the real cost in 1938.(44)

It is clear from these figures that as late as 1955 a substantial proportion – in 1959 it was twenty-one per cent of the total – of the increased expenditure on education went on the social rather than the educational needs of the schools. It boils down to this: can we afford this expenditure on such things as heavily subsidized school meals when we are still without adequate school buildings, enough school teachers, or properly equipped laboratories?

Do we actually look upon education as an investment at all? British governments, whether on the 'right' or 'left', do not. For instance, a debate on education in the House of Commons draws much less attention from the Members than a debate on the Licensing Laws. We suggest, though we like our glass of beer, that the education of the nation is a great deal more important than the amending of these laws. Why does the demand for private education rise all the time? Because there is a widespread belief that we shall never have a really first-rate system of state education in this country. The state schools will improve; that is not denied. But it will always be too little and too late. We will keep up with other countries, or nearly so, but we will never be in front of them. We will provide places for children in schools, but we will never take the next step and also provide first-rate education.

How urgent is the need for an adequate investment in education? We believe that on it depends our survival as a nation of fifty million people, with a rising standard of living, able to play its part in the world of the next forty years. Recently the Ceylon Government advertised again and again for a water engineer in England. She failed to receive a single application, so she turned to Russia and found herself with a choice of twenty-five well-qualified men. What is true of our failure to send qualified men overseas is true of our failure to find even enough qualified men to meet the tasks at home. This may be a historic moment. We have been overtaken in education by many nations who were formerly behind us. Very shortly we shall be both overtaken and out-distanced. In a world which no longer owes us a living we cannot afford to waste the immense talent, much of it still latent, which belongs to our race. For the fact of the matter is that we have wasted this talent in the past. We are, for instance, paying the price today in all walks of life for the scandalously inadequate system of secondary education which existed in Britain before the last war.

Are we prepared to invest in education? If we scrap one weapon we invest in another; and we invest at once. If we have a secondary school without a qualified teacher of mathematics or science we do not act with the same urgency. But in the long run the penalty for failure to act may be greater in this case than in the first. The first fault can be put right; the second cannot. We are a rich nation and we want to become richer. We are an influential nation and we want to continue exercising our influence in the world. We need to use our greatest capital asset, our men and women, to the fullest possible extent. We must therefore offer them first-rate education. Nothing else will do.

The *sine qua non* of a first-class system of education is a first-class teaching profession. We can build new universities and technical colleges; we can design modern schools and equipment; we can organize an entirely new concept of secondary education; but without an adequate supply of teachers of quality the whole thing will fall to the ground. To what extent are we investing in such a supply?

The problem of quantity is a question of getting qualified teachers of mathematics and science. It is a different problem as between the boys' and the girls' schools. In the maintained grammar schools alone the demand has considerably outrun the supply since 1953. Senior pupils in these schools have increased in number since that year by about twenty-five per cent, graduate teachers have increased by seventeen per cent, mathematics and science graduates have increased by fourteen per cent. And this takes no account of the non-selective schools where the position is much worse. A recent survey undertaken by the Headmasters' Conference reported as follows on the replies received from just over 1,000 secondary schools:

> In the last year 23 independent, 19 direct-grant, and 290 maintained schools had had vacancies which they could not fill, or filled unsatisfactorily. Thirteen independent, 8 direct-grant, and 181 maintained schools had had vacancies unfilled for a term or more.(20)

Even in the grammar schools it is difficult to get mathematics graduates; the position is undoubtedly much worse in the secondary modern schools.

It is more difficult still for a girl to obtain a good education in mathematics and science. A recent survey was also undertaken by the Association of Headmistresses:

In some 800 schools, mainly grammar with a sprinkling of secondary modern, there were 320 vacancies for mathematics staff last year. There was no applicant for seven per cent, only one for forty-one per cent. Some fifty-seven per cent were filled with complete, and twenty-three per cent with partial, satisfaction. In nine per cent the appointee was completely unsatisfactory, and eleven per cent were not filled.(21)

There are even schools, usually in the north of England, where there has been no qualified head of the mathematics department in the school for years at a time.

Furthermore, the figures quoted above apply largely to the independent, direct grant, and maintained grammar schools. These schools do not cater for more than a quarter of the secondary-school population. Precise figures are not available, but it does not seem very likely that the non-selective schools, which educate nearly three-quarters of our children, are adequately staffed with mathematics or science graduates even to the extent of having a graduate to organize the teaching of the subjects in the school. And in the training colleges from which many of our secondary teachers come there is still a grave shortage of qualified lecturers in mathematics and science. In 1956, for example, in a survey of seventy-five women's training colleges, there were found to be fifty-four which had no mathematicians or scientists amongst their lecturers.

Underlying the whole problem of the quantity and quality of the teaching profession is the question of salaries. Many observers of the educational scene have found it incredible that successive governments, which have had a definite policy for curing deficiencies in school facilities and buildings, have had no such policy for attracting an adequate supply of good teachers. In contrast, the independent schools have long believed that the priorities should be reversed and that the buildings must take second place to the teachers in the demand for investment. Before 1944 a state system of secondary education did not exist in Britain. So long as a minority of children – the scholarship winners – were the only ones to receive secondary education, it was possible to recruit secondary teachers on the cheap. In the 1930s, a time of great unemployment, the education authorities had a buyers' market. They used it to good effect in recruiting a large number of graduate teachers who today still form the backbones of many schools. Since 1944, however, there has been full employment and a sellers' market, and, in addition, the number of secondary school children has of course increased enormously. Quite without logic, post-war governments, committed to establishing a system of secondary education for all children, have failed to appreciate that it is no longer possible to recruit teachers on the old terms. The result, as Crowther clearly showed, has been a steady decline in the quality of graduate teachers.

A popular national myth has also been at the service of governments reluctant to face the problem of recruiting teachers. It goes by the name of 'vocation'. Teaching, says the myth, is not quite the same as other people's jobs. It is a 'vocation'. We don't really want to compete with other salaries in the open market (says the myth), because if we do we probably won't get the right sort of person. A good teacher has a 'vocation' for teaching: we don't want the kind of person who is only looking for a good salary. And so it goes on. The peculiar thing is that the myth is contrary to the practice of every other profession and of the business world. Teachers are just as human as everybody else – even school children can be convinced of this – and they are not prepared to sacrifice a way of life and a standard of living to become teachers. They expect to receive a salary not less than that which is received by people of equivalent intelligence and qualifications engaged in other professions or occupations.

Do they in fact receive such a salary? In a recent memorandum on teachers' salaries some interesting comparisons were made. A two-year trained teacher (now to be three-year trained), having Advanced Level G.C.E. in two or three subjects, would receive after nine years' service the pay of a married senior corporal in the Regular Army. At about the age of thirty-seven, he would reach his maximum salary, which would be about the equivalent of a well-paid charge-hand in industry.

Having reached his maximum of £1,000 he can look forward during the rest of his teaching career to further bonuses not exceeding an extra £105, unless he becomes a headmaster or a deputy headmaster.

Again taking our figures from Burnham salary scales current in 1961, a four-year trained teacher, holding a Third-Class or General Degree and a Diploma of Education, would reach his maximum salary at about thirty-nine when he would receive £1,090. He has superior qualifications for which he has taken two additional years of training and for which he receives a paltry differential of £90. In fact the two years' salary, which he has missed by taking two years longer over his training, is only made up to him after twelve and a half years of service. Clearly there is not much incentive here for being better qualified.

What are the prospects for the highly qualified men and women? A teacher who holds a First- or Second-Class Degree (i.e., a good Honours qualification) may start on a par with his similarly qualified contemporaries in industry or commerce. But his starting salary contains the only major advantage which he will get over the less well qualified teacher. This is because he receives the same increments as everybody else in the teaching profession. Therefore, with fixed annual increments of only £27 10s., he rapidly falls behind the Honours man in other jobs until, by the age of thirty, his position no longer compares favourably with industry or commerce. Small wonder that at this stage, when family burdens are beginning to assume larger proportions, the Honours Degree man very often seriously considers leaving the teaching profession.

Finally, how do we value teachers in positions of great responsibility? A department head, responsible for the standard of work, say, in English, in a school of 600 pupils, is paid less than the salary of any moderately successful businessman at the age of forty. The deputy headmaster of such a school, responsible for the time-table, receives very little more. And the headmaster, responsible for the education of 600 children and for the leadership of about thirty teachers, receives less than an army major and almost £1,000 a year less than a general medical practitioner. Furthermore, it is not so very long since a survey of head teachers' salaries estimated that only ten per cent of head teachers received a salary of more than £1,500. The memorandum concludes with these words:

> If we compare this [the head teacher's salary] with the salary of a company director, a high-ranking Civil Servant, a medical specialist, or a leading man in the legal profession or the armed services, the teacher is quite clearly in a vastly inferior position.[4]

Such is the nation's estimate of the head teacher.

One further point should be made. The teaching profession has access to few of the 'extras' that sweeten the salaries of other professions. There is no free travel or accommodation, there are no meals free or on expenses, no gifts or the use of cars, no subsidized clubs or sports: there is not even a very advantageous pension scheme – as many teachers' widows know to their cost. The teacher has to live on his salary – and his salary alone.

If one way of recruiting a first-class teaching profession is to offer adequate salaries, another way is to offer professional training comparable with the other professions. The requirements for such training are that it should confront the trainee with a stimulating course in both academic knowledge and practical teaching experience; that the qualification achieved should be the equivalent to graduate status, even though it might not be achieved in the three-year period at present required for a first degree; and that such training should be considered essential for everybody seriously intending to make a career in teaching. In Scotland such professional training has been provided for many years. In England and Wales it does not yet exist for two reasons: first, because our degree-giving bodies, the universities, are incapable of providing it; and second, because governments have so far been unable to give training colleges for teachers the necessary authority and status to achieve such a standard on their own. In practical terms this means that the nation is content that there should be an ever-widening gap between the independent, direct-grant, and better-known grammar schools, which absorb the limited number of university graduates, and the secondary modern schools, which are staffed largely by the men and women from the training colleges. The graduate has been trained to degree standard; he therefore has a qualification which is valuable on the labour market whether he decides to teach or not. The training-college student has been trained to the much narrower qualification of being considered to be a trained teacher; he has a qualification which is marketable only within the educational world. This is the cause of the gap.

If we are to attract people into teaching, we must be prepared to publicize education. It is extraordinary that a minor academic matter – the question of whether or not Latin should be a compulsory requirement for entrance to Oxford and Cambridge – should attract more nation-wide publicity than any House of Commons debate on the education of the country. It is amazing that amidst all the elaborate brochures, produced under the aegis of Her Majesty's Stationery Office and financed by the British taxpayer, there is scarcely one pamphlet which sets out in imaginative form the purposes and achievements of secondary education. It is rather odd that, when so many of the people engaged in 'education' are employed solely on administration, the teacher sending in his application for a post is required at the same time to include a stamped, addressed envelope if he wants a reply! No wonder that in 1959 the City of Birmingham, faced with an acute shortage of teachers, realized that traditional methods of recruitment were hopelessly inadequate and decided to advertise widely in the national Press.

Finally, we must abolish the ridiculous regulation which limits the earnings of pensioners if they 'teach', but allows them to earn as much as they can if they do some other job. This regulation treats retired teachers thoroughly shabbily and is unworthy of a cultured community. It is a legacy from the bad old days when the main concern of governments was to keep education 'cheap' irrespective of the quality of the education that was provided.

To the question – Are we investing enough in our teachers? – the answer returned is a decisive 'no'. Neither do we provide an adequate salary scale for them, nor do we provide professional training. The foreseeable results of present policy will be an increasing amount of ever more mediocre education until at some date in the not far distant future the nation, which must pay the bill, will revolt at the low standards of achievement and abandon the great experiment of 'secondary education for all'. To put the matter into a headmaster's own words:

> I must insist that one good teacher (that rare thing!) is worth ten good syllabuses. And if thousands of pages have been devoted to this subject for every ten on syllabuses, so much the better – for this way lies salvation.

We turn now to the other and less important half of the area of educational investment – the investment in the building and equipment of schools. Rare praise was lavished on British architecture at the recent International School-Building Congress in Milan. Many delegates noted the close contact which has existed since the war between the architects who design our schools and the men and women who work in them. It is likely that next year this congress will meet in London because, as an Italian put it, 'it is the place where the buildings we admire most come from'. Much remains to be done before every child in Britain is in a school built no earlier even than the beginning of this century. Particularly important is the fact that progress in school building has not kept pace uniformly throughout the country. Nevertheless, there seems a reasonable chance that by the mid-1960s the vast majority of our school buildings will be better built, more roomy, and more comfortable than ever before.

But when we turn to the equipment of schools it is a different story. In 1949 laboratories were commonly inadequate. In 1958, nearly a decade later, *The Times Educational Supplement*, discussing this question in a comment on the June issue of the *School Science Review*, said, 'It is a sorry tale of skimped benches, neglected pipettes, and plain administrative folly.'[61]

The same issue of the *Review* showed that at a most generous estimate only forty-four per cent of grammar-school laboratories came up to the Ministry of Education's standards – and these standards themselves are considerably lower than those allowed by the Industrial Fund for the Advancement of Scientific Education in Schools. Since 1958 the deficiencies in the grammar schools have been largely remedied by increased expenditure. But the loss to Britain of two school generations of potential scientists cannot be put right. Why, one asks, did expenditure on laboratories not keep pace with other sectors of educational expenditure? Are we now to make the same mistake in secondary modern schools? A recent survey of science teaching in these schools, carried out by the Science Masters' Association, reported that: 'Accommodation is "grossly" inadequate. Fewer than half have properly equipped laboratories; in some there is no running water.' (37)

There is a contrast here that is of the utmost significance for British education. It is the contrast between the splendid exteriors of our new schools and the comparative inadequacy of our investment in the mental processes for which they exist. The BBC have pioneered the way in educational television since 1957, yet out of 30,000 schools no more than 2,500 are equipped to receive the programmes. A film-strip projector is not yet part of the normal equipment of every school in the country. West Germany currently spends £170,000 on the use of films for teaching in schools: our expenditure is £9,000. Educational film development has proceeded at a greater pace in Scotland than in England and Wales.

> In 1939 [says Professor Andrew Buchanan] 3,150 Scottish school departments possessed about 378 projectors – twelve per cent of all schools. In England and Wales, with their 31,000 grant-aided schools of all types (including training colleges), there were about 1,400 projectors – four and a half per cent of all schools.(8)

As a nation which publishes over 480 new books every week, are we really satisfied that the total annual expenditure on all school-books runs at £1 18s. per year per child in secondary schools? How many schools have a tape recorder? How many schools have a record player with which to make use of the increasing numbers of excellent linguistic recordings? Is it fanciful to suppose that we are just a little bit old-fashioned in the way we respond to these new media? 'All very well' (one can almost hear a voice in the staff-room) 'all very well these things for foreigners – but we don't want these new-fangled devices in English education!'

Everybody knows that English education is a little bit like show-jumping with the height of each hurdle raised for the decreasing number of competitors. How much money are we prepared to invest in order to ensure that each of the examination hurdles is the fairest and most accurate test of the competitor's ability? Professor Eysenck argues that the most formidable of all the hurdles, the 11-plus examination, could be made more accurate. He points out that a single intelligence test on a single day, which is the basis of the present system, provides no way of assessing the capacity of the child for growth. At the same time it lends itself very strongly to 'cramming', which is highly undesirable in the primary school. He argues that a more accurate assessment would be to conduct five hours of intelligence testing at intervals throughout the child's primary-school career. This would enable a most reliable growth-pattern to be kept for each child which would almost certainly provide a more accurate assessment of the child's potentialities. Why, he asks, is this not done?

The reason is a very simple one. If it costs 9d. per child to give one test of intelligence and score it, then it would cost almost 4s. to give five tests. The decision that a child's future happiness is worth only 9d. rather than 3s. 9d. is not made by the psychologists, but by the general public through their elected members of local government bodies. All one can say is that for 9d. the public is getting quite incredibly good value for its money. To have a fairly superficial examination of a car carried out costs several pounds. A reasonably complete health examination costs at least as much. To get a child's intelligence investigated for 9d. can hardly be considered extravagant expenditure. During my recent visit to California I was shown a large series of laboratories constructed at a cost of several million dollars for the sole purpose of getting a few thousandths of one degree nearer to absolute zero temperature! Our society is willing to pay large sums of money like this for a slight increase in the accuracy of physical measurements, but it is content with the expenditure of 9d. a child in the measurement of a psychological variable of great importance to both the child and society.[19]

New examination procedures – and they are badly needed at all levels and not only at that of the 11-plus – will mean educational research. Towards the conclusion of his Report Sir Geoffrey Crowther drew attention to the fact that there was an almost total absence of information upon which such research could be based. He used the word 'pitiable' to describe the amount of money currently spent on research in relation to the annual education bill of this country.

Concluding our survey on the current amount of money which the public is prepared to spend on educational investment, we come to the broad field of culture. The Arts Council, which dispenses nearly a million pounds annually, believes in a policy of building up the quality rather than the quantity of artistic work. For example, it spends over half this sum on the national opera and ballet, a further large sum on music, and in 1957–8 it had the miserable sum of £55,500 with which to sustain the whole of the rest of the arts – painting, sculpture, poetry, festivals, arts centres, and clubs, as well as literature, architecture, and film for which the Council cannot really attempt anything at all. It is scarcely surprising that such places as the British Museum are among the least attractive museums in the world. But then, as an expert in this field has said, 'Britain has the lowest government contribution to the arts of any civilized nation.'[5]

We have produced our evidence. The nation's education is still run on the cheap. There is no reason why Britain, whose only remaining capital asset is in the talent of her men and women, should not spend as much per child on education as does the United States of America – at least as much. Such expenditure should be regarded as the best long-term investment that Britain can possibly make for the future. Without such investment we foresee nothing but decline, beginning with a decline into mediocrity leading finally to poverty – poverty of mind and poverty of resources.

The ability to think ahead is the distinctive mark of intelligence. What kind of return may we expect from a substantial investment in education? Recently a 'Panorama' programme on education produced what the BBC described as a flood of correspondence'. The programme had shown a private cramming school which catered for the 11-plus examination and achieved a seventy-five per cent pass-rate (i.e., passes to grammar schools). As a result of the original programme and the correspondence, about twenty of the writers were invited to come to the studio for interview in the following week's 'Panorama'. From the two programmes two entirely different points of view emerged: the parents of the children were almost unanimous in their approval of the cramming school which neglected almost all forms of real education; the correspondents who appeared in the studio the following week were almost unanimous in their rejection of this school and its methods. Perhaps it is also significant that a large proportion of those interviewed were teachers. Both groups, however, were very much concerned with the quality of education; the parents certain that their child would get a better chance in a grammar school, and the correspondents concerned that a protest should be made against such a travesty of education.

The first return on our investment will be a large increase in the numbers of qualified people. A minority of them will be qualified as scientists, technologists, or technicians. For the majority of people, however, what will be needed will be the quality of 'general mechanical intelligence'. As Crowther pointed out, we must have people who are prepared for very rapid change in the conditions of their work. The job which a child will start on today may have ceased to exist when he retires from work in the next century. The processes and machines with which he will be working at the time of his retirement may not yet have been put on the drawing-board. He will probably have lived through at least one technological revolution in his industry. His training, and in particular his mental attitude to his work, will therefore need to be entirely different from the attitudes which still largely prevail today and which are based upon a previous industrial age when a man, trained in one mechanical skill, would spend a lifetime practising that one skill. 'Clearly,' as the Report says, 'the first quality that is needed to cope with such a world is adaptability.' (44) On the question of training boys and girls in 'general mechanical intelligence', we shall have more to say when we discuss the teaching of science (see Chapter 4). We must draw attention now to the inadequacy of our investment in higher education.

'One of the starkest statistics in the whole of English education' (44) is Crowther's comment on the fact that only one out of every eight young people between the ages of sixteen and eighteen is still receiving full-time education. The Crowther objective that in twenty years' time fifty per cent of this age-group should be in full-time education is modest indeed when compared with the fact that there are industrial nations which already aim at a figure of a hundred per cent. Figures about higher education speak for themselves, as may be seen from Table 1.

These figures indicate the relative position of our post-school education. Small wonder that on 13 January 1961 *The Times Educational Supplement* asked in its editorial, 'Have we now enough brains to plan the strategy of the race and in time to catch up and challenge the leaders?' for nothing less than our survival as an independent nation is at stake.*

But a large increase in the total number of places available in full-time education will be insufficient without a revolutionary effort to provide adequate part-time education during the immediate post-school years. After a century or more of neglect, the government have now initiated such a policy. Its success will be judged by whether the children who leave school

* Government policy now aims to provide 170,000 university places by 1973–4. In its editorial leader of 20 May 1962 the *Sunday Times* described this number as 'quite inadequate'.

Table 1 *Number of University Students in Different Countries*

Country	*Number of students in universities*	*Population (in thousands)*	*Approximate number of university students per million population*
U.S.A.	2,918,212	175,000	16,670
U.S.S.R.	2,013,565	200,200	10,000
Argentine	142,000	20,060	7,100
Australia	61,879	10,000	6,190
Czechoslovakia	79,235	13,287	5,960
New Zealand	12,507	2,244	5,570
Poland	139,244	27,500	5,060
Romania	81,206	17,490	4,640
Canada	72,745	15,970	4,550
Finland	18,765	4,356	4,310
Italy	212,424	50,000	4,250
Bulgaria	31,134	7,630	4,080
Spain	117,722	29,089	4,050
Yugoslavia	72,267	18,387	3,930
France	170,023	43,854	3,880
East Germany	64,497	17,300	3,730
Switzerland	16,531	5,160	3,200
West Germany	151,343	50,594	3,000
Austria	20,863	7,000	2,980
Belgium	25,169	8,950	2,810
Egypt	63,761	22,651	2,810
Netherlands	30,939	11,094	2,810
Denmark	12,447	4,448	2,800
Portugal	22,319	900	2,480
United Kingdom	*90,500*	*49,812*	*1,815*
Ireland	7,670	4,295	1,790
Turkey	42,642	24,000	1,780
Norway	5,952	3,511	1,690

Source: Unesco, *International Yearbook of Education*, 1957, U.N.: H.M.S.O., London, 1958.

Do so-called Universities have the same standards in all countries??

at fifteen or sixteen, and are not suitable for a place in a university or a college of advanced technology, nevertheless feel that they have an equally good chance of obtaining technical qualifications under part-time release. We have rejected, rightly in our view, the expensive American solution of offering college education to every boy or girl. This rejection, however, will prove fatal unless the 'alternative' part-time route is clear, stimulating, and well signposted.

The second return on our investment will be a more cultured and civilized community. In fact, if we believe in our way of life and if we make the claim that its basis is respect for the individual man and woman, it is very difficult to see how we can be content to invest in education only just over half the percentage-rate that Marxist Russia does. It is also very difficult to see how we can rest satisfied until every child in the land, irrespective of the geographical accident of his birth or the affluence of his parents, has *a chance*. An equal chance is, of course, an absurdity. Unfortunately the arguments which have been lavished on so-called equality of opportunity have obscured the fundamental question that there should be opportunity for everybody at every stage in education.

Why must we become more civilized? Because we have embarked in this century, and not until this century, on an experiment in mass-representative democracy. Pious talk about an educated electorate is meaningless unless the electorate has been educated to vote intelligently and resist political propaganda. In 1960 democracy received renewed impetus during the famous Kennedy–Nixon debates on television, when a great democratic nation sat down to watch a serious discussion about its future. Elections in Britain likewise have always been considered a time for serious debate on the state of the nation. But as the old issues, like unemployment, recede, we shall be faced with issues likely to be less clear-cut and demanding greater powers of reasoning. The functioning of democracy will become more difficult as the speed of change increases. The possibility of lowering the voting age to eighteen will undoubtedly be a topic of the next decade, and this can scarcely be considered without an investigation of the general educational level of the country.

Schools are directly responsible for the culture of the nation. Crowther referred to the rapid expansion of the mass media and the fact that it bore heavily upon boys and girls during their most impressionable years. The effect of the media is to atrophy rather than debase our culture. There is also the encouraging fact that there is a minority of the media that strives unceasingly to raise our cultural standards. Our culture is compounded of a unique mixture of the Christian and the rationalist traditions, the 'Hebraic and the Hellenistic' of Matthew Arnold. Both are necessary for our civilization and both are now engaged in the process of re-interpretation. On more than one occasion in the past, the uniqueness of the two traditions has surprised our friends, bewildered our opponents, and astonished ourselves. Both are now challenged by the barbarism of an unadulterated technology.

There is therefore the political problem, the cultural problem, and lastly the intellectual problem. 'Education with inert ideas', said Professor Whitehead, 'is not only useless; it is above all things harmful.'[74] Schools are faced with the immensely difficult task of handing on the ideas of the past, tempered by the experience of the present, to the men and women of the future. The effectiveness of education cannot, except in the most superficial sense, be reckoned by the numbers of children who pass a certain examination. A much fairer test would be to ask to what extent the pupils of a school, when they reach in middle age positions of influence in the community, still retain receptiveness of mind and combine it with maturity of judgement. For schools are responsible for the intellectual inheritance of mankind. Apathy is the one inexcusable failure of a school. Probably it does not matter very much whether the ideas which are produced in a classroom gain an immediate and enthusiastic acceptance or arouse a vigorous if short-sighted opposition, but it is a serious matter if they provoke no more than passive resignation on the part of the pupil. For, once the mind has been aroused, the main part of the job has been done.

We return to the plea of this chapter and this book – that Britain has never yet cared to invest money in her one remaining capital asset, her men and women. Her rate of expenditure on education has consistently lagged behind that of her main industrial rivals. Hardly a responsible politician since Disraeli has dared to face the central issue – if Britain wants to catch up with the rest of her competitors she must invest money. Not even the extravagant heroism of two world wars can conceal the fact that the efficiency and the quality of Britain have steadily declined in this century. For far too long state education in this country has been run cheaply, with results that can be clearly seen today: too few teachers of too low quality; too many boys and girls chasing too few opportunities in higher education; too little concern with the training of enough scientists, technologists, and technicians; far too little concern with the principles of education, backed by too paltry a sum of money for educational research; too little effort to persuade the nation of the value of good education. Totally inadequate investment in the past has left us in the predicament of today.

Early in 1961 *The Times* devoted a leader to the state of Britain. This is what it said:

Why did Britain's exports increase between 1958 and 1960 only half as much as Germany's or Sweden's and less than a third as much as Italy's, France's, or Japan's? Why have her export prices risen the most? Why has her production risen less than half as much as continental Europe during the last eight years? These shortfalls are more than enough to account for all the balance of payments difficulties since 1955. Due allowance must be made for the late start made by Germany and Japan, for Germany's special accretion of manpower, and for France's devaluation bonus. But after all that there remains a large element of simple failure which cannot be explained away except in terms unflattering to the national ego. Figures corroborate what foreigners say and what most of us privately admit – that Britain's economic life has been falling behind in vigour, ingenuity, industry, and imagination.... Taxation apart, Britain suffers from a deeply ingrained defensive mentality, a static conservative mood which assumes both a man's right to go on selling the same amount of the same goods as in the past and a man's right to a good job in the same town as his father.(58)

The Times is by no means the only journal which has seen in recent years in Britain a country that has lost its national purpose.

The loss of purpose, the complacency, the 'couldn't care less' attitude of Britain is not the result of a little more prosperity; after all we have often survived bursts of prosperity in the past. This loss of purpose is quite simply due to the fact that since 1945 Britain's place in the world has changed more radically than almost any other nation's, but that her mental outlook has not changed with corresponding speed. So, as of many fields during the last fifteen years, future historians will say of Britain that she acted 'too little and too late'. A large part of this mental time-lag can be attributed to the inadequacies of our educational system. A substantial investment in education now would be the most economic way in which we could insure ourselves against a continuation down the path of the last fifteen years. In fact it is the only way in which we can insure ourselves for the future, because it is the only way in which we can make certain that our greatest asset, the skill and character of our people, can be fully developed.

What kind of education should we invest in? The rest of this book is an attempt to answer this question.

CHAPTER 2

The Needs of the Child

WHY is there a contrast between the splendid exteriors of our new schools and the inadequacy of so much that goes on inside? The building of personalities is both more exciting and more complicated than the construction of schools. We shall start by considering the needs of the child and the society to which the child will soon belong, and build up from first principles the fundamental aims of secondary education.

When considering the ideal content of education one of two approaches is usually adopted: either the structure of the curriculum as it has been traditionally built up is critically investigated, or an attempt is made to construct a list of needs of the child using as a basis only ethical principles and the existent civilization in which we live.

The latter course, which we intend to adopt, is more exciting but more dangerous. Especially dangerous for us because we attempt it in one chapter and pose only seven questions from whose answers we shall extract the basis of our curriculum. Exciting indeed – 'How do I want my child to be brought up?' 'What sort of life should he be prepared to live?' 'What should he be taught at school?' – this chapter is a look at principles and an expression of aims.

There are some who argue that the content of the curriculum is less important than the methods by which the child is taught. We do not agree. The nineteenth-century curriculum was built firmly upon the theory of 'transfer of training'. This school of thought, dedicated to the use of such terms as 'mental discipline' or 'formal training', believed that the intelligence could be trained with such effect in one field of study that it could then be applied without further training to any other field. Lord

Milner, for example, one of the most intelligent men of his generation, was called upon to tackle the problem of the unification of South Africa after receiving a higher education largely devoted to the writing of classical verses. Today we have reason to wish that he might have been somewhat better prepared. Even when 'transfer of training' was established, it is hard to see why, with the limited resources available to education, more care and time was not spent in finding a curriculum which satisfied true educational needs as well as providing a mental discipline.

Research has shown clearly that 'transfer of training' does not take place to anything like the extent that it was believed to in the nineteenth century.

> Improvement in any single mental function rarely brings about equal improvement in any other function, no matter how similar, for the working of every mental function-group is conditioned by the nature of the data in each particular case.(46)

There is in fact very little automatic 'transfer of training' even amongst the ablest pupils, and probably none at all amongst the less intelligent ones.

On the basis of this research the content of the modern curriculum assumes an importance which it never had during the nineteenth century. For, with the discrediting of the theory of 'transfer of training' and with the extension of education to a wider range of intellect, it becomes of paramount importance to balance the curriculum in such a way that all the vital mental and moral faculties can be trained. And, if this training is to achieve a wider vision and understanding than the mere acquisition of factual knowledge of subjects, then great efforts must be consciously made to relate one subject to another.

We must be concerned then not only with *how* we study but also with *what* we study. It is one of the dangers of the traditional approach to the curriculum that the *matter* taught is accepted and only the *manner* in which it is taught is criticized.

It has been suggested 'that all teaching is biased in favour of the world of yesterday rather than the world of tomorrow; that we teach the truths of 1920 to the men and women of 1984'.[40] In this climate of opinion radical experiments, such as the eight-year study recently undertaken in thirty leading American high schools, rarely receive the attention they deserve. A tremendous amount of ink and paper is devoted to the detailed organization of our schools, but surprisingly little is written about what the schools ought ideally to be teaching. We think this is due to the national belief in muddling through. The curriculum has become almost too sacrosanct for the reformers. It has been endowed with traditional qualities which are regarded as too important to be tampered with.

Some authors have compiled, in much greater detail, longer lists which have much to commend them; but we are after fundamentals here and, at the risk of a loss of detail, our list of seven questions concerns the needs of the school-leaver and the needs of society. The list is intended to indicate only the ideal minimum of educational objectives which should govern the reform of the present content of education and bring it up to date. We do not think that secondary education needs complete re-thinking – if it does, one book will hardly suffice – but we think that it has been overtaken by the very rapid changes in society. Our aim is to show how it can be adjusted not only to the needs of the present, but also to the needs of the future. It is because we must prepare for the unknown future that we cannot draw up a more specific list. For the future will belong to the flexible person who is more prepared to ride with events than to oppose change.

The seven questions are as follows:

1. How far has a child been enabled to develop his own personality?
2. Is our education an adequate preparation for becoming a good citizen?
3. Is the present system of physical education satisfactory?
4. What contribution can education make to the responsibilities in the home?

5. How effectively can the school-leaver communicate?
6. How skilful is a child when he leaves school?
7. How well equipped is a child when he leaves school to become a self-supporting member of the community?

1. How far has a child been enabled to develop his own personality?

The majority of parents send their children to school with the conviction that the school will make something of them. They feel that the years spent at school, almost irrespective of the subjects which their children study, will contribute powerfully to the making of the man. But intellectual training by itself is no more than part of the necessary preparation for maturity. Character training is essential and

> in our concentration on academic performance we lose sight of our main business of educating human personality. We engage ourselves strenuously in the certification of plumbers, but give scant thought to developing men and women of moral character.(62)

Personal realization cannot be achieved without moral purpose. During adolescence children are confronted with the problem of 'what constitutes good and bad conduct'; with the problem of 'how to distinguish between right and wrong'; with the problem of 'how to decide between duty and pleasure' – and other fundamental moral problems. The curriculum that is not specifically designed to bring these problems before the child is inadequate. Because, until the child has been made aware of what is expected of him in the development of his character, he will not be capable of beginning the task of self-discipline. Sir Philip Morris claimed that the present curriculum was at fault because it lacked any such moral purpose. In his view all consideration of the curriculum should consider 'how best to use subjects for the purpose of education . . . rather than regarding education as the by-product of the efficient teaching of subjects'.(33) Until education is conceived as a whole process, in which body, mind, and soul are jointly guided towards maturity, a child's personality will not necessarily be developed.

Within the classroom it is the humanities which provide the

clearest guide to the problems of morality. It is difficult to see how moral purpose can be brought into education without continuous study of religion, philosophy, literature, and history. The fact that half today's sixth-formers are virtually debarred by the current system of specialization from ever studying these subjects in the sixth form is a serious defect in the curriculum. For what other way is there of discovering the underlying values of our civilization? Few would deny the majesty of English literature in the cultures of the world, and foreigners must be astounded to find that it sometimes plays a comparatively minor part in English sixth-form education. Future generations may find it curious that, whereas the Regius Professorship of Greek was founded at Cambridge in 1540, the Chair of English Literature was not established until 1910 – but then English is not considered as good a discipline as Greek! Until English is reinstated to its rightful place in the curriculum, generations of children are being deprived of their heritage.

The way in which a child carries out his work can be influential in the development of his personality. Somehow he needs to gain a sound knowledge of his capabilities and limitations, of his good and bad points. There is no reason why initiative – for that is what it amounts to – cannot be fostered inside as well as outside the classroom. Outside the classroom he has to learn to play his part in a variety of activities, all of which are related to the purpose of his education.* Inside the classroom there is the project method of teaching him. This method is essentially a method of learning by doing.

> It is rightly claimed that this method touches the springs of action most directly of all. There is hardly a child who will not go into action with alacrity when it has been decided to set up an exhibition with the title 'Blanktown – Past, Present, and Future', to be open to visitors in a month's time and to consist of models, paintings, posters, animated diagrams, maps, plans, and real objects, all mounted on boards and tables round the classroom walls.(35)

A project such as this, in which each member or two members of a class have a clearly defined part to play, presents the child

* See page 41 for a discussion of extra-curricular activities.

with the nearest approach to an individual challenge of initiative that is possible within the classroom. Because it is work which he himself has chosen to do (within the framework of a preconceived plan) he will work with a responsibility which he does not always feel for more formal teaching. This responsibility is the very quality which he will need to be a really effective member of an organization in adult life. A project also has scope for the expert which does not always exist in the classroom, where the pace of work must depend to some extent on the other members of the class. Challenged to find out all he can and present his work as attractively as possible, a child will apply to it all the concentration of which he is capable, and in the end he will gain the most satisfying feeling of being the 'expert' in the field. And expertise provides a sense of confidence and critical evaluation without which the mind cannot develop. For these reasons the project can help him to develop his personality.

As a child approaches maturity he needs opportunities for choosing between different courses of action with their various consequences. This implies that the sixth-form curriculum should contain a number of 'elective' * subjects. It also implies that the sixth-former should be allotted an adequate amount of private study time to read around these subjects. The years from eleven plus to fifteen plus are inevitably largely occupied with the learning of mental skills, for these are the indispensable tools for later performance. But when he enters the sixth form a child has to learn to develop his own 'point of view'. He has, in fact, to learn to think as a grown-up person; to understand general ideas and concepts, to detect complicated fallacies in a chain of reasoning, and to develop his own line of argument. For this is the *raison d'être* of sixth-form education. In its discussion of the sixth form the Crowther Report had this to say:

> The years in the sixth form are crucial years in which the foundations of a sound social and moral judgement can be laid.(44)

* The American word for an optional subject of study.

It is no exaggeration to say that the sixth form is the turning-point in the development of personality, and that many of the values which a child establishes at that time will remain with him for the rest of his life.

We may summarize the discussion on the development of personality by indicating that it is a matter of discipline and freedom. The discipline is one of morals, in the study of which a child learns to match his own ideas and conduct against certain criteria of right and wrong until he reaches the point where he begins to establish his own standards and values. The freedom is one of action in which he is encouraged to work with imagination and responsibility towards goals that he, himself, has accepted as valuable and worth while. In the sixth form a child can attain a maturity which will stand him in good stead for his entry into adult society.

2. Is our education an adequate preparation for becoming a good citizen?

What are the qualities which a child will need in order to be able to play his part in the life of the community? What kind of knowledge must he have at his command if he is to participate in the life of a democracy? Can we equip him to take his place in our complicated democratic society?

Modern societies, especially those like our own which live and work in exceptionally crowded conditions, depend on co-operation. If the environment of the school, and in particular of the classroom, is based primarily on the concept of competition, it is unlikely that a child will be greatly interested in what can be achieved by cooperation. Competition does not often encourage a sense of social responsibility.

> Surely in education the emphasis should be on activities of which the pupil continuously sees the point – activities which are either delightful in themselves or means to valuable ends which the pupil has accepted. Competition distracts attention from all this. It shifts the emphasis from what is intrinsically valuable to what can be marked.(11)

A measure of competition may have its place in the classroom as being the only method by which one teacher can stimulate thirty or forty children simultaneously. But there should certainly be equally energetic attempts outside the classroom to encourage cooperative effort.

> School societies are so important in helping maturity and independence to blossom that, if for one reason or another they cannot meet after the school day is over, room may need to be made for them by lengthening the lunch-hour or by arranging that the school day finishes altogether at 2.30 or 3 on one afternoon a week, though the children will not of course go home until the usual time.(34)

In fact, activities which were once regarded as peripheral to the serious work of the classroom should now be brought within the school curriculum. Every child should be involved in at least one of these activities and the emphasis should be always on the amount of cooperative effort which he is prepared to contribute. Working – in any capacity – on play, orchestra, opera, magazine, film, or exhibition, he will learn to lose self-interest by contributing to the corporate interest. For a great many children, and more especially those who do not excel in the academic work of the classroom, this may be the most valuable experience of their school career.

A school must also take active steps to provide democratic experience. By this we do not mean merely that it should organize its clubs and societies in democratic forms, although this is important. We mean that the discipline of the school should be orientated towards a respect for the individual. Every child should feel that he and his work 'count' and that he is making a contribution towards a larger whole. Discipline there must be, and every school will have occasion from time to time to exercise the power of authority. A completely free system is based on a profound misreading of human nature. But such exercise of authority should always be the exception rather than the rule. Democratic experience requires that individuals should be faced with the challenge of freedom.

Knowledge of democracy is essential for the school-leaver. A child needs an understanding of our political and legal system and he must be able to compare it with that of other countries. He also needs an appreciation of the economic foundations upon which the various political systems are based. It is of considerable importance that this knowledge should be made both lively and interesting. Democracies seem to be far more likely to perish from political apathy than from any other cause. Therefore his enthusiasm must be aroused. In the teaching of politics, law, and economics, in a very real sense, 'all knowledge is contemporary knowledge'. This has been clearly realized by the Marxist historians of contemporary Russia whose teaching is based upon the premise that the history of Russian political institutions before the Revolution is irrelevant to an understanding of Russia today. We must convey a sense of vitality and experiment in our politics, while retaining our traditional links with the historical past.

Contemporary society is moving away from nationalism towards internationalism. We live in 'one world' in which the old-fashioned nation-state can no longer operate as an independent unit. It is no more than the bald truth to say that we must unite or perish. The forms which unity will take are still barely perceptible. But certainly we must make greater efforts than we have in the past to understand our neighbours. In a recent broadcast Mr John Sharp suggested that a new view of teaching history will be needed:

> I must not argue that there is no place for the history of the past; but in the short time available I wonder how much a boy can afford to give to agricultural medieval England. He is going to see very little trace of it around him. Instead the balance of trade, the emergence of nationalism in Africa and Asia, the struggle to develop the industrial resources of the world will, or should, occupy his attention. If history is to mean more to him than a picturesque set of legends it should help him to understand a serious newspaper.[31]

As Mr Sharp has suggested, the growth of international understanding is largely a question of the emphasis which is given to such work in the curriculum. In the past it has often received the time available when other needs have been met. In the future it will require a greater priority.

Whether education should be centred on the needs of the individual child or on the needs of the community has been debated since the time of Plato. A great deal has been said in recent years about the needs of the child – to the benefit of education. Now is perhaps the time to re-formulate and re-assert the needs of the community. In this section we have drawn attention to these needs.

3. Is the present system of physical education satisfactory?

Some facts should be known concerning the legend that we are a nation of sports lovers. In 1959 the National Playing Fields Association estimated that seventy-five per cent of children leaving school at the age of fifteen took no further part in any active sport or physical recreation. As everybody knows, only private generosity enables Britain to be represented at the Olympic Games. During the last war, as one of our correspondents has reminded us, the physical fitness officer in the Armed Forces of the Crown was a figure of fun and his work considered to be of little importance. And finally we might take note that it was not until the General Election of 1959 that any political party considered that the government should spend money on providing sporting facilities for the public. And so we have 'a nation of sports lovers in the paradoxical position of being worse equipped in the basic amenities than many of the countries to whom we exported our games and sports'.(62) It is against this national setting that physical education takes place in the schools.

First of all, a child needs that degree of general fitness which will enable him to exert a continuous physical effort over a long period of time; in short, he demands as near-perfect health as he can get. A good boarding-school lays claim upon his most formative years and undertakes to train him in the habits most likely to bring him such health. But for the majority of children who never leave home to go away to school more formal instruction in health and hygiene are necessary. For instance, a boy must be convinced of the necessity to take care and trouble over his muscular development as he would over anything else – hence the new ideas of Circuit Training which have proved effective in many schools. He must also be instructed in personal hygiene, and towards the end of his school career this instruction should include such topics as smoking and the effects of alcohol upon the body. A boy also needs to be familiar with elementary First Aid and the signs and symptoms of the most common illnesses.

Secondly, a child should be introduced at school to the possibilities of physical recreation. Great strides have been made in recent years by such bodies as the Central Council for Physical Recreation in adding to our meagre facilities for sporting relaxation. Pastimes which used to be the prerogative of the leisured and the wealthy are today the practice of the general public. For example, ten times as many skiers seek the slopes now as they did twenty years ago; sailing clubs are full, moorings being almost unobtainable; Rugby Union teams are increasing year by year and even providing colts sides for the old boys of secondary modern schools who, at fifteen, are too young for senior Rugby. In Wales and Scotland there are growing opportunities for climbing in the mountains and a big demand for the Outward Bound Courses which follow closely the original ideas of the Gordonstoun scheme. There is no evidence of a falling away from the traditional English games of cricket and soccer. The possibilities for physical recreation are increasing and the school should do all in its power to persuade its pupils to take part.

Physical education, as our correspondent pointed out, flourished in antiquity and decayed during the Middle Ages. Its renaissance in England has been delayed until this present century. In many ways it is the most easily met of all the needs of youth because of its very practicality and self-sufficiency. It still suffers in this country from woefully inadequate grants of money. However, physical education has recently received an enormous fillip to its status by its inclusion as a degree course at Birmingham University. Today physical education is firmly established as an essential part of the secondary-school curriculum.

4. What contribution can education make to the responsibilities in the home?

The successful family life is the most envied accomplishment of any man or woman. Significantly, it has been the first institution to come under attack in a state such as Nazi Germany. All that is said about the stability of family life in the pulpit or in the Press is undoubtedly true. Happy, purposeful families are the greatest force for good which can be enjoyed by any community of people. Everything that we have said about the moral purpose of education and everything that we have said about the development of the individual child will have its bearing when he faces the task of building a family of his own. This indeed is one of the main reasons why education is a process of far greater complexity and importance than the learning of various subjects and techniques. Families cannot be built upon half-baked personalities.

> If the family is to be as secure in the future as it has been in the past (and we can be content with nothing less), there will have to be a conscious effort to prepare the way for it through the educational system on a much greater scale than has yet been envisaged.[44]

Such was the recommendation of the Crowther Report. The 'mass media', as the report pointed out, bear very heavily upon the teenager. With all the skill of applied psychology the media focus upon the teenager at a time when he is neither boy nor man, but when he is already a wage-earner and consumer – at the time when he has just left school. If he is to find his way through this difficult period and reach the goal of a happy marriage and home he will need what the Report calls 'some counter-balancing assistance'. The foundations of such assistance must be laid at school.

In the transitional stage in which society finds itself today, it is the task of the school to face up to the problem of developing the right curriculum for girls as well as boys. A curriculum that fails to develop the femininity of girls, that either treats girls to a series of 'soft options' or merely offers them a watered-down version of the boys' curriculum, cannot fail to have the most serious repercussions upon our homes. The modern girls' curriculum must also take into account the earlier age at which girls marry and their consequent desire to return to a part-time career when they have borne their children.

Recently a head wrote in *The Times Educational Supplement* about the kind of way in which sex education could be tackled amongst the older pupils:

> In these days of teenage marriages it does not require a great stretch of imagination to see the school-leaver as a potential family man. Sex biology lessons by the science master with the willing assistance of the school medical officer have led eventually to a consideration of the relationship between human physiology and the conventions of society, and ultimately sex and family relationships.(60)

These are the sort of foundations for which the Crowther Report pleaded.

'Manners makyth man', runs the old saying, and there is no reason why a child should not learn the ordinary social graces while at school. To a great extent these are things which the day-school child will pick up from his observation of contemporary society. But he will be a much nicer person in his home, whether as child or parent, if he has developed a proper approach, for example, to his encounters with women, visitors, or older people in general. It is not unreasonable to hope that by the time he approaches his late teens he will be able to move without embarrassment in most walks of society. From a practical point of view he should be taught to realize that subsequent employment may depend to some extent on his acquiring such facility.

The teaching of sociology has a part to play in preparing young people for the responsibilities of home life. To know how other people live, in other countries as well as in one's own, is a broadening process. To be able to compare their way of life –

their customs, their houses, their entertainments, and their points of view – with one's own cannot but be beneficial. Educational exchange is certainly of value here. Such exchange will be far more valuable if it has been preceded by some preparatory teaching about the country to which the children are going. In a different way the study of social topics from a historical viewpoint can be of use. In both cases the child's outlook should mature from such experience.

5. How effectively can the school-leaver communicate?

'Why can't the English teach their children how to speak?' sings Professor Higgins in *My Fair Lady*. Why not indeed? How archaic were those educationists of the nineteenth century who considered reading and writing to be more important than speaking! We should learn our lesson from Nazi Germany where a supremely skilful orator succeeded in seducing a supposedly highly educated nation. Effective speaking is by far the greatest boon that any school can bestow upon its pupils. To be articulate enables a person to explain his ideas; to express his feelings; to persuade others to a course of action. With the growing complexity of society it is becoming more and more important that men and women should speak with clarity and poise. And allied to the power of speech is the power of listening to other speakers. The skilful listener will save himself much wearisome perusal of printed matter during his lifetime. He will be at home in the world of the mass media.

Oral communication involves the most basic of the basic skills necessary for living in society. Speaking and listening, though not included in the three R's, are far more important than any of them, and a school which fails to teach its pupils to speak easily and effectively and to listen intelligently is guilty of a gross dereliction of duty.(35)

The particular forms of our way of life are in fact bound up with effective speech. Parliamentary democracy may prove to be this country's greatest contribution to the advance of civilization. Other nations have succumbed to demagoguery but we still give the accolade to the man or woman who can make his mark in a committee of his fellows. The qualities which he needs are the same, whether he is speaking in the House of Commons, the council-room, the board-room, or the cricket club. It is perhaps no accident that the visitor to London so often goes first to watch the oratory on a Sunday afternoon in Hyde Park. Our freedom of speech is the most richly prized of all our freedoms.

Reading and writing remain skills of tremendous value in contemporary society. Today, however, they must be more widely interpreted than in the past. The written word, which was once used almost exclusively in literature and political documents, has now become the source of a vast mass of information on every conceivable subject. Ability to survey such information – whether it be in book, pamphlet, manual, or timetable – and to extract the relevant matter, has become of great importance. At the same time it is of equal importance for anybody to be able to express himself with considerable clarity on paper. Professor Parkinson has pointed out the necessity for properly worded notices of vacancies for jobs if the advertisers of the post are to avoid wading through a host of totally unsuitable applicants. And there is no doubt that initial selection for many posts in business and the professions depends upon the skill with which a person can fill up a form. In all these ways as well as in the more traditional literary work of the schools, to which we have referred, there is need to teach the skills of reading and writing.

The art of communication, therefore, constitutes the first of the basic skills which should be taught to a boy in school. This was clearly recognized in a notable American educational report:

> In a free and democratic society the art of communication has a special importance. A totalitarian state can obtain consent by force; but a democracy must persuade, and persuasion is through speech, oral or other. In a democracy issues are aired, talked out of existence or talked into solution. Failure of communication between the citizens, or between the government and the public, means a breakdown in the democratic process.(25)

6. How skilful is a child when he leaves school?

With the first uncertain steps around the perimeter of the play-pen, the child begins to learn the immense range of skills which he will require for his life. From his schooling he can expect to receive most of the basic mental skills which he will need. For the justification of compulsory education is that a school is far better equipped to train the young mind than any other institution. The type of education by experience that was picked up successfully by Huckleberry Finn is no longer adequate for a child's needs. Unfortunately perhaps, in some respects, there is little chance today for the self-educated person. In the foreseeable future there is no escape from the process of organized learning for anybody who wants to take his place in the modern world. For there are certain mental processes which must be absorbed steadily and systematically, beginning in early youth. These processes constitute the basic mental skills.

Crowther makes it quite clear that no one can expect to attain 'numeracy' at school who has not studied mathematics and science 'up to roughly Ordinary Level [G.C.E] standard'.(44) The Report distinguishes two different aspects of numeracy:

> On the one hand [it] is an understanding of the scientific approach to the study of phenomena-observation, hypothesis, experiment, verification. On the other hand, [it] is the need in the modern world to think quantitatively, to realize how far our problems are problems of degree even when they appear as problems of kind.(44)

And the Report goes on to stress the importance of numeracy:

> Numeracy has come to be an indispensable tool to the understanding and mastery of all phenomena ... the way in which we think, marshal our evidence, and formulate our arguments in every field today is influenced by techniques first applied to science.(44)

Numeracy, therefore, is the ultimate aim and, combined with literacy or the power to communicate, it constitutes the most important basic mental skill. The school-leaver at fifteen or sixteen will not be 'numerate' – on account of his youth. But by that age he should have received the necessary grounding in mathematics and the natural sciences to enable him to progress towards numeracy, with further training. In the course of this grounding he will have learnt mathematics, of great importance for almost any job which he may undertake in later life. In the sciences he will have grasped the essential features of the material world. From both mathematics and science he will have experienced the value of accurate observation and precision, and thus his mind will have gained the elements of a scientific approach to intellectual matters. As a basic skill numeracy is of prime importance for the child in the twentieth century, since 'the man who is innumerate is cut off from understanding some of the relatively new ways in which the human mind is most busily at work'.(44)

From numeracy, the skill, *par excellence*, of observation and critical analysis, we turn to 'creative ability', the latent talent which lies in every human being. The strains and stresses of the Industrial Revolution, as William Morris pointed out, largely destroyed the old opportunities for 'arts and crafts'. School curricula, faithfully reflecting the philosophy of its day, followed suit.

> Until twenty years or so ago [a recent article put it] few secondary schools in this country did more than provide a few weekly lessons of drawing and painting, and woodwork was almost the only craft offered.(15)

We may add that when secondary schools finally awoke to the fact that the development of creative ability was a fundamental purpose of any education which claimed to educate the whole person, this type of education was still considered irrelevant for the able child. That it was considered irrelevant was due to the undue predominance of the old literary tradition.

Because of the eclipse of the teaching of 'arts and crafts' in secondary schools, children are at the moment given few opportunities to develop creative ability. In the curriculum of the able child this kind of work is still considered to be of only peripheral interest.

A boy may be asking that he should be taught to do, as well as to appreciate, what others have done. He wants, perhaps, to play in an orchestra, and not merely to listen to one; to paint and not only to receive lessons in art appreciation. He stands in a tradition many thousands of years old, an educational tradition, though not historically a school or university tradition. It is a task of importance to make this other tradition of artistic or creative education (historically a matter of professional or technical training) *as much a respectable part of the general educational system* [own italics] as the largely analytical tradition of the schools. It is right to add that some of the most encouraging educational achievements of our time have been precisely in this sphere.[44]

We believe that this kind of education should be an essential part of a secondary-school curriculum. Equipped with skills of this kind a child has resources which will stand him in good stead in the future. Not only will he be able to add colour and variety to his immediate surroundings, but he will also be able to make better use of some of the leisure time that is increasingly likely to come his way.

We conclude that a primary purpose of secondary education is the teaching of certain basic skills. The art of communication, or literacy, is the first of these skills. The attainment of numeracy, or 'an understanding of the basic nature and aims of science', is the second. The third is the discovery and training of creative ability.

7. *How well equipped is a child when he leaves school to become a self-supporting member of the community?*

Modern society ensures that all his life a child will have to live on a limited, taxable income. Money is the symbol of independence and there are few greater thrills in life's progress than the day when the first pay-packet is received. In recent years our society has also been paying school-leavers on a scale never envisaged twenty or thirty years ago. An education which has not included sound advice in the use and management of money must be considered an inadequate education. This is a matter of bread and butter. But there are greater issues at stake.

Money is also the symbol of the material world and its needs. If the school has not developed an approach to the monetary values of this world, the school-leaver may soon find himself in the midst of anxiety and even great unhappiness. And lastly, monetary values underlie the basic economic facts of the wider world. Nobody in this century can ignore the worldwide problems of rich nations and poor nations, developed countries and underdeveloped countries, citizens and refugees. A child who has begun to understand the value of money will be able to appreciate the need for charity.

And so to his choice of career. Sir Oliver Franks writes:

> Much depends upon our young people. When the range of opportunity is so wide it is most important that they should, as far as possible, choose the right career: right for their own future happiness and the development of their talents, and right because it enables them to make the best contribution to their community.(13)

The choice of career is the first really important decision that a child has to make and a school bears a good deal of responsibility to ensure that he or she does not make a blind choice. Indeed, this responsibility is considerably increased by the prospect of longer education for many boys and girls in the future. Whether the school-leaving age will be raised to sixteen, or whether the length of full-time education will be extended by more voluntary staying on at school, a great deal of efficient, up-to-date guidance on careers will be needed. That this will necessitate a reappraisal of the curriculum is made clear from a recent report to the Nottinghamshire Education Committee by a study-group of head teachers and industrialists. The group, which was convened to consider the advice currently given by schools on careers in industry, reported:

> It is essential that teachers should have a more intimate knowledge of industry than the vast majority seem to hold at the present time.... Such information should influence the teaching of older pupils and the courses provided for them.(6)

Of the one-and-three-quarter million boys and girls in the fifteen to seventeen age-group in the year 1957–8, not more than one-seventh found their way to courses of further full-time education – at universities, colleges of technology, or similar institutions. In fact, in that year (1957–8), Crowther estimated that not more than two-fifths of the fifteen to seventeen age-group were receiving education of any kind whatsoever, full-time or part-time. Over a million boys and girls of this group were already working full-time on the adult labour market. The majority of school-leavers, therefore, start their working lives when they leave school, and schools cannot avoid playing their part in preparing boys and girls for this life. It is significant that such work on the part of the schools was specifically recommended as a matter of priority in the very able Report produced in 1955 by King George's Jubilee Trust:

> We are sure that this responsibility of the school to prepare its pupils for work, which will occupy the greater part of most days, as well as for leisure, involves a re-examination and eventual re-formulation of our national educational policy and curriculum, both as regards school life and the early years at work.(30)

Angry young men with ability have become figures of fun for the social cartoonists. But we should remember that many of them were most angry about their schooling. They were angry – and rightly so – because they had not learnt at school to look ahead and make a realistic estimate of the future. They had not been taught to consider their future position in the community in relation to their own abilities, aptitudes, and desires. They had not realized that their education represented an investment in the future which might not pay off in the early years. In any such consideration of the future the value of money and the choice of a career should be two essential topics in the curriculum of every secondary school.

Our list of seven questions about the fundamental aims of secondary education for the able child is now concluded. There are, of course, many more aims which would be generally accepted by anybody who has anything to do with secondary education. But we believe we have reached a point today where secondary education is in danger of splintering into fragments under the pressure of many conflicting claims upon the limited time available. Therefore we think it is extremely important to establish the 'major' objectives of the curriculum. These objectives, we believe, should be determined by two, and only two, criteria: (1) The needs of the child who is preparing for adulthood; and (2) the needs of the society in which the child will have to play his part when he reaches maturity. Against these criteria we have compiled our list.

CHAPTER 3

The Purpose of the School and the Origins of the Present Curriculum

SCARCELY a day passes without somebody writing a letter to some journal suggesting that 'more education' is what the nation needs. There is rarely a conference assembled to discuss any topic which does not conclude its proceedings by voting in favour of 'more education' to solve its particular problems. And no responsible government in the world today can afford not to give its blessing to a policy of 'more education' for its people. Education has become the slightly miraculous panacea. And so the letters are written, the conferences assemble, and the governments pronounce: 'more education' is what the people want; 'more education' is what the people will get. 'More education' becomes the answer to the shortage of scientists and technologists; 'more education' will of itself produce more trained personnel (whatever that may mean); 'more education' is what is needed by the sixteen to twenty-two age-group; 'more education' will bring down the divorce rate; finally, consciously stated or subconsciously believed, 'more education' will make us top nation again. Thus the schools become involved in a multiplicity of aims and objects connected to a greater or lesser extent with the real aims and objects of education. But, unfortunately, having tried very hard to satisfy these multitudinous purposes, there is then little time left to consider the true purposes of bringing children to school.

Schools exist in order that children may be led forward from childhood to the threshold of maturity. The influence of a school, good or bad, should be a lifelong influence. It should be lifelong because children are in the care of schools during some of their most impressionable years. Schools should be second only to family life in influencing, for good or evil, the development of character during adolescence. The quality of the school community will be the first impression which the child will have of the society in which he will ultimately have to take his place. It may well be the decisive impression. The way in which he is treated by other people and the way in which he learns to treat other people will have a great deal to do with the habits and attitudes which he developed at school. His general approach to the topics which will concern his generation will have been influenced, positively or negatively, by the way in which these topics have been approached at school. His methods of working and the way that he uses his leisure will both reflect the way in which he worked and played as a child. In these and in many smaller ways the influence of the school is decisive.

Nothing is more instructive than the clear realization by the Marxist states that education must have a purpose behind it. For Marxist education is probably the most single-minded education to emerge in the world since the Reformation. It reflects in its entirety the purpose of its founder:

> His mission in life was to contribute in one way or another to the overthrow of capitalist society. Fighting was his element and he fought with a passion, a tenacity, and a success which few could rival. He died, beloved, revered, and mourned by millions of revolutionary fellow workers, from the mines of Siberia to the coasts of California, in all points of Europe and America. His name and his work will endure through the ages.(2)

Indeed it has already become apparent that the Marxists have had considerable success in deliberately propagating Marxism through the Russian education system. Like the Nazis they have shown how generations of children can be effectively indoctrinated, provided the entire resources of the state's schools are used for that purpose. The lesson of Marxist education, however, is not that we should ourselves devise a narrow system of ideas which should be taught in every school. It is rather that we should examine the philosophy upon which our education is based, a philosophy which is immensely richer than Marxist philosophy, and that we should then make sure that the education which we give to our children does in fact express our philosophy.

Not so very long ago T. S. Eliot pointed out that Christian presuppositions account for the major part of our heritage. For example, by far the greatest movement of opinion in this century in Britain, the whole range of beliefs which underlay the movement towards Socialism and the Welfare State, was profoundly Christian. So deep and heartfelt were these ideas that today they have become part of the accepted basis of our society. Many of the great reforms of the last century, of which the most notable was the part played by Britain in the abolition of slavery, were directly due to the influence of the Christian religion. When the leaders of all the churches wrote their famous letter to *The Times* (Foundations of Peace), they were doing no more than reminding us of the fact that England was a Christian country. The position was accurately summed up by Mr Chuter Ede, during the House of Commons debate in 1944, when he said: 'Most parents want their children to have a grounding in the principles of the Christian faith as it ought to be practised in this country.' To whatever extent these Christian presuppositions may be redefined over the next half-century they remain the basis of the English heritage.

It is a fallacy to assume that boys and girls can be brought up in a spirit of academic agnosticism. Theirs is pre-eminently the age of heroes and gods. And the greater the pressure which bears upon their intellectual and emotional development the more necessary is it that life should have a purpose. Field-Marshal Montgomery was right when he argued that 'we have got to make it clear that they have something to be proud of in the past, and something to do in the future'. [55] If there is a spirit of pettifogging cynicism abroad in this country today it is merely because nobody has tried, since Winston Churchill, to remind the British people of these things. We have, after all, a great deal to be proud of and a great deal still to do. If ours is indeed the age of analysis, it is surely equally true that it is an age requiring constructive action on a scale more generous and far-reaching than at any time in the past.

We argue therefore that the purpose of a school is to provide for the needs of the child and that other aims are subordinate to this purpose. And we argue that because the heritage of this country is a Christian heritage our education must be conducted on Christian presuppositions. We do not think that the problem of the secondary-school curriculum, to which we now turn, can be solved on any other basis.

The school curriculum is central to all other problems of secondary education. Are we teaching the right things? Why, for instance, do we put up with the steady emasculation of the English language until it reaches a point where even the universities begin to complain that the standard of English of those sitting for first degrees has declined significantly? In a wider context, why are we content to allow our language to be taught all over the Asian and African world by Russians who speak it better than we do ourselves although they have never set foot in England? Why have we become, as an Australian put it, 'charitably indifferent' to our Commonwealth – and bored and ignorant too? Why have we almost missed the tremendously exciting challenge of science to the extent that a secondary-modern schoolteacher can say that

> they [the pupils] did not believe they could ever learn 'science'; that, in any event, science was not for them; that they could never make a living out of knowing any science. Science, in fact, was 'the end'.(37)

Why is there no effective political opposition, and why has an election been won on the banal slogan of 'You've never had it so good'? And why do we put up with an endless stream of war memoirs, war films, and war commentaries all designed to focus our minds upon the year 1942 rather than the year 1962? We cannot today plead the rigours of austerity to justify our backward-looking. Have we simply gone soft?

If we are just out of date in the way we think about the world, is it not conceivable that part of the trouble may be that our schools are dedicated to an out-of-date curriculum? Out of date rather than deliberately false like the Nazis' or the Marxists'. Because as much damage can be done in a school curriculum by what is put in as by what is left out. The time is limited and for the majority the end of schooling still marks the end of general education. Of course there will be much more vocational training; of course there must be in the future far more widely spread further education for everybody; but nevertheless basic general education will go on ending for most people at somewhere around fifteen or sixteen. At that age they will already have most of the general ideas which will be theirs for life. Minds which are not at that stage already opened to the world of today will not easily open later on. What we have to ask is whether our present curriculum is designed, specifically, to achieve such an end? Has it been so carefully planned and considered that it does in fact provide an education for 'today' and 'tomorrow', for '1962' and for '1984', or does it exist as it is merely because of its inertia and tradition?

The curriculum of English secondary schools grew up in a manner different from the curriculum of schools in other countries. At no point in history did the state intervene to order what should be taught in English schools. Indeed, a perusal of the last great English Education Act – the 1944 Act – would not reveal in any one of its 122 sections any directive about the subjects which should be taught in schools. A visit to Ministries of Education in other countries might often reveal what is being taught in the schools on that particular day, even perhaps at that particular hour. Not so in England, where the state is required to provide the framework of education, the teachers, and the schools, but not to determine what is taught to the children.*

Neither the Minister nor the Local Education Authority exercises authority over the curriculum of any school beyond that of agreeing the general educational character of the school and its place in the local educational system.(52)

* Except that the 1944 Act required that in all primary and secondary schools there should be a daily corporate act of worship and that religious teaching should be given.

Today this freedom from state interference in determining the school curriculum is the most richly prized asset of English education. We must look elsewhere for the origins of the present curriculum.

This curriculum – we might call it the traditional curriculum – is based on three ideas, all of which have been influential during the last hundred years. First, there is the literary tradition which was the offspring of the Renaissance and which provided, through the medium of Latin and Greek literature, the link between the ancient and the modern world. Secondly, there is the scientific drive which began with the realization, as a result of the Great Exhibition of 1851, that England must struggle hard in the field of technology if she wished to retain her commercial and industrial position in the world. And thirdly, there is the influence of the progressive philosophy of education which originated with Rousseau, reached the primary schools with Froebel, and was incorporated in the 1944 Act when the Act required that local authorities should provide education according to the 'age, aptitude, and ability' of the child. We shall examine each of these three basic influences.

To illustrate how these basic influences have come to determine the present curriculum we have drawn up a timetable in Diagram 1, page 63. It is a timetable which is familiar to the majority of secondary schools where there are children who are working for the Ordinary Level of the General Certificate of Education. Because the content of English education is determined by no single centralized authority, there is of course no single timetable which can be called the timetable of a secondary school. Therefore this timetable can be only an approximation, but it is, nevertheless, the sort of timetable to which most secondary schools adhere if they teach to G.C.E. O-level standards.

From the Renaissance until the present century the literary tradition dominated English education. And during the whole of that period the language that was considered to be the literary language *par excellence* was not our own English language but Latin. This was more true of the old-established grammar schools than of any other schools. For who can forget the celebrated statement of Lord Chancellor Eldon in 1805, in a lawsuit concerning the introduction of new subjects at Leeds Grammar School, when he upheld Samuel Johnson's definition of a grammar school as 'an institution for teaching grammatically the learned languages' and gave judgement against the teaching of French, German, mathematics, or anything but Latin and Greek in the school? During all these years a mastery of Latin was accepted uncritically by many teachers as the primary objective of the secondary-school curriculum.

The general effect of such thinking almost proved disastrous for English education. Its most grievous effect was the fact that it was not until modern times that serious study was given to the teaching of the English language itself. In 1921, after no less than fifty years of compulsory elementary education in this country, the Board of Education published a report on the teaching of English:

> From the evidence laid before us it became speedily clear that in many schools of all kinds and grades that part of the teaching which dealt directly with English was often regarded as being inferior in importance, hardly worthy of any substantial place in the curriculum and a suitable matter to be entrusted to any member of the staff who had some free time at his disposal.(3)

A glance at the present curriculum (Diagram 1) shows that we have not yet installed English language and literature in their rightful place. Of the total time available each week no more than a quarter – nine periods – is devoted to English and the associated subjects of history and geography. Now everybody is agreed that a primary aim of education in the years between eleven and fifteen is to provide boys and girls with a good general background of the customs and traditional culture of their own country. Such a background can be provided only through the medium of their own language and literature. When the culture of their own country happens also to include what many people regard as the greatest language and literature in recorded history, it seems well-nigh incredible that English receives so little time in the curriculum. For a knowledge and enthusiasm for English should lead inevitably to a study of the English legal and political system, which is perhaps our distinctive contribution to contemporary civilization. At the same time a common language enables boys and girls to study in detail the history and culture of the American people; for the first time in modern history it is thus possible to compare two contemporary cultures through the same medium. And at the same time the study of English today is the study of a language which is likely to become the international language of half the world.

The first, and most extraordinary therefore, of the legacies of the classical literary tradition has been our failure to install the English language as the very core and centre of the secondary curriculum.

There is an authentic story of a statistically minded German professor who worked out the total number of punishments he had inflicted in a teaching career of just over fifty years; these, he tells us, included over 900,000 strokes of the cane, of which 800,000 were for 'Latin words'. During its long hegemony the teaching of Latin became for the most part ever more narrow in outlook and more grammatical in approach. There can be few more curious episodes in the long history of education than the way in which the *grammaticus* of ancient Rome, the conscientious analyser of the Latin text, cast his shadow into the future. It is remarkable that 'there was not a great difference in the teaching of Latin and Greek between nineteenth-century Eton and the schools of Imperial Rome'.(9)

Such emphasis on grammar has profoundly affected the study of foreign languages in England. A living language, if it is to be effectively taught to children, must emphasize the art of speech just as much as the art of writing: a dead language can only be concerned with the art of writing, which is largely a question of accurate grammar and syntax. Therefore our superstitious reverence for the grammar of a language favoured – for centuries – the study of Latin as against the study of the

Diagram 1 *'Old-Type' Curriculum*

PERIODS

1 2 3 4 5 6 7 8 9 10 11 12 13 14 15 16 17 18 19 20 21 22 23 24 25 26 27 28 29 30 31 32 33 34 35

11+ to 13+	13+ to 15+	15+ to 17+
Latin	*Latin*	*Specialist Subject No. 1*
French	*French*	*Specialist Subject No. 2*
English	*English*	*Specialist Subject No. 3*
Mathematics	*Mathematics*	*Non-Specialist Subject*
History	*History*	*General*
Geography	*Physics*	*Religious Knowledge*
Nature Study	*Chemistry*	*Physical Education*
Art	*Religious Knowledge*	
Music	*Physical Education*	
Religious Knowledge		
Physical Education		

AGE 11+ 12+ 13+ 14+ 15+ 16+ 17+

modern languages. The facts speak for themselves. In 1914 there was still no Professor of French at either Oxford or Cambridge. In 1956, out of a total number of candidates in French, German, Latin, and Russian at G.C.E. O-level amounting to approximately 150,000, only ninety-one sat the examination in Russian. And there are still many secondary schools in England where it is impossible for a child to learn more than one modern foreign language. How important, for instance, may the South American market become to this country in the immediate future? But how difficult it is for a child to learn to speak Spanish really well at school! Despite great progress during the last thirty or forty years we have still much leeway to make up in the teaching of modern languages.

Without more ado we must now claim the time allocated to Latin (see Diagram 1) for more worthwhile ends. We do not believe there is any substance in the argument that Latin is unequalled as a mental discipline. If transfer of training does not exist (see page 35) it would surely be more worth while to train minds linguistically either by an intensive study of English or by an intensive study of a language of the future rather than of the past. For those who want to study the ancient world as a great culture and civilization it would surely be more sensible to start the study of Latin as an optional language in the middle school or in the sixth form. The fact that Latin ceases to be a part of the timetable for every child will in no way diminish the opportunities for the study of the Greek and Roman world. In how many schools where Latin for all is retained is there a significant correlation between its study and the far more important study of Roman civilization? If time were no problem, we could retain Latin in a modified form for its most significant linguistic attribute – as background knowledge for English words. But this is not reason enough for its retention. Some of our correspondents have suggested that a general linguistics course could achieve this end without the use of so much time.

The present curriculum, therefore, reveals the influence of the classical literary tradition which dominated English grammar-school education from the Renaissance to the present century. This great tradition is now obsolete as a vehicle for secondary education. Its legacy is the conviction, firmly held in our secondary schools, that the study of language must be one of the main purposes of intellectual education. It is this conviction which we must now bring up to date.

What has been the effect on the school curriculum of the introduction of science over the last hundred years? In the first instance the Great Exhibition sparked off a debate between the proponents of scientific education and their opposers. No less a personage than Dr Arnold himself led off for the traditionalists:

> Rather than have Physical Science the principal thing in my son's mind, I would gladly have him think that the Sun went round the Earth, and that the Stars were merely spangles set in a bright blue firmament.(54)

Such was the opinion of one of the greatest headmasters of the nineteenth century. T. H. Huxley and Herbert Spencer took every opportunity to urge a scientific basis for education. In a powerful plea for the study of both the natural and the social sciences Spencer attacked the method of teaching languages by the excessive use of memorization. In contrast to the *authority* of teacher or author, he suggested that it was the *judgement* of the pupil which was the true aim of education; this power of judgement could come only from the learning of scientific method. Looking at the record of history he wrote:

> While what we call civilization could never have arisen had it not been for science, science forms scarcely an appreciable element in our so-called civilized training.(54)

Despite such argument many of the leading educationists of the nineteenth century opposed the introduction of science into the curriculum with all their might and main.

The fact that science has had to fight for its place in the curriculum against the opinions, often frankly anti-scientific, of many educationists has had lasting effects in this century. In the first place the broad and fascinating field of natural science as an integral part of the curriculum has given place, especially in the sixth form, to a rigid specialization. Until very recently no serious attempts have been made by the universities or by examining bodies to curtail the amount of factual knowledge in the interests of maintaining the broad curriculum. The Norwood Committee noted, in fact, that in 1942 a university scholarship paper was comparable to a tripos paper of twenty years before. In the main body of the school no serious attempts have been made until very recently to teach a sufficiently broad concept of general science to the majority of pupils who will never become science specialists. It is as if science, responding to the years that it spent in the wilderness, is now determined to go its own way and build up the walls round its own castle.

Secondly, and resulting from the way in which science was merely added to rather than integrated into the curriculum, has come the now-famous concept of the 'two cultures'. In Sir Charles Snow's opinion the plight of the arts specialist is far worse than the plight of the scientist. It may not be impossible for the scientist to acquaint himself with the literary, artistic, and musical culture of the world, but the arts specialist has in all probability been left high and dry by the rapid progress of scientific thought. Referring to these unfortunate people, many of whom are the leading intellectuals in this country, he said in his Rede Lecture in 1959:

> So the great edifice of modern physics goes up, and the majority of the cleverest people in the Western world have about as much insight into it as their Neolithic ancestors would have had.[53]

The integration of scientific training into the general education of secondary schools – the numeracy to which we referred at the beginning of this book – is perhaps the most urgent problem of the curriculum. About sixty per cent of the Praesidium of the Supreme Soviet are estimated to have received enough scientific training to enable them to follow the implications of rapid scientific progress and to foresee future developments. Of the 335 M.P.s in the 1958 Parliament who held university degrees, 295 held arts degrees, leaving only 40 to be divided among scientists, doctors, and veterinary surgeons. It is extremely probable that many of the arts-degree M.P.s finished their scientific education at the age of fifteen or thereabouts. Are we equipping our rulers for the modern world or for a world of our imagination which ceased to exist about the time of the Battle of Waterloo?

The problem of training children in numeracy is primarily a sixth-form problem. In Diagram 1 we have shown how, under the existing specialization, a child may quite easily cease all further scientific education on entering the sixth form. He may well have received a solid course in elementary science in the middle school, since quite a large number of periods is usually allocated at that stage. Now this elementary course will, of necessity, be both stimulating and at times rather trying for the mediocre child. Its whole *raison d'être* lies in the fact that it should be continued, like all elementary courses, to the point where he can begin to comprehend the application of the elementary principles which he has already learned. But under rigid specialization this is precisely what he cannot do. When he enters the sixth form all his energies are immediately transferred to his specialized arts subjects.

Progressive education has so far been applied more to the methods of teaching children than to the content of their education. Its major premise has been that children learn most effectively when their interest is aroused, and that their interest is most efficiently aroused by making them participate as much as possible in the process of learning. It has caused, in many schools, a welcome variation from the strictly didactic methods used for so long in the classrooms. Its most successful development has undoubtedly been the project method of teaching (see page 38). For many pupils it has made education a great deal more worth while. Very often it is possible to enlist children's interest by appealing to more senses than the older methods of memorization followed by reiteration.

But a glance at the time-table indicates that subject-mindedness, the traditional approach to the curriculum, has remained basic to the secondary school. The various subjects remain carefully isolated in their various compartments, and usually isolated in the mind of the child. There is neither time nor place in the present curriculum for the introduction of new subjects or the grouping together of established subjects in such a way as to give the child any notion of the unity of knowledge or its relevance to contemporary society. The demands of the subject, greatly accentuated, as we shall see, by the examination system, have remained the over-riding feature of the secondary curriculum. Once the classics provided such unity and generations were nurtured not only on the classical languages but also on the whole scale of classical values. With the ending of classical education there has been no unifying factor to take its place.

Such are the features of the present secondary curriculum. Our contention is that this curriculum is largely the result of tradition modifying itself in the course of this century. Its two most archaic aspects are the prevalence of the grammatical tradition which has prevented adequate study of the English language and the rigid division between the arts and the sciences which has dispossessed about half our ablest children of their scientific inheritance. This curriculum has never been re-assessed from first principles, nor has it been re-evaluated with reference to the kind of world in which our children will live in the latter part of this century and the early years of next century. For all the talk and print that have been expended on the organization of our schools, very little thought has yet gone into the content of the curriculum. We want to build up a contemporary curriculum which will meet the needs of the child today and in the future.

CHAPTER 4

A Curriculum to Suit the Needs of the Child: The Needs from Below

HOW can we plan such a curriculum? We propose to work very closely from our list of seven questions and to devise a curriculum to meet these needs.

In a secondary school there should be a broad rhythm in a child's education. For the first two or three years the curriculum should express the needs of the child as an individual, ignoring largely the demands of the community outside the school. These needs we will call *the needs from below*. At the age of thirteen to fourteen there should be a change. Now the curriculum should be concerned to a greater extent with the demands that society will shortly make upon the young adult. These demands we will call *the needs from above*, and these needs will become more important after the age of fourteen. In this chapter we shall consider four of our seven questions which concern the needs of the child during the early years; in the next chapter we shall consider the three questions which concern the needs of the child during the later years. From the discussion of all seven questions we shall derive a 'new-type' curriculum for secondary education. This curriculum is illustrated in Diagram 2 on page 98.

How far has a child been enabled to develop his own personality?

Personality must be developed through the humanities. By the humanities we mean art, music, religion, philosophy, narrative history, local studies, and English culture. All these subjects form a unit of study for a child during his early years at a secondary school. Treated as such a unit they are to him the natural extension of what he learnt in the later years of his junior school. Provided he has not been crammed for the 11-plus examination in such a way that he no longer appreciates the humanities as a whole, he will have no difficulty in accepting this unit of study. For with the humanities we are concerned with the imagination and the romance of life; and these are qualities which are experienced intensely during these years. That is why it is a mistake to treat the humanities subject by subject at this stage. Destroy this unity, substitute for it a series of subjects taught with little relation to each other, and you destroy a part of the imagination and curiosity with which the child is liberally endowed at this age. Squeeze the humanities into a corner of the curriculum and you will achieve the same destruction.

From eleven to thirteen nearly half of the curriculum should be devoted to the humanities – an extra period every day on the present curriculum. In addition to this there should be further time devoted to studying the grammar and syntax of the English language which we shall consider under the problem of 'communication'. The old classical curriculum devoted as much time and more to the study of classics, thus making it the core-subject of the curriculum. As much time will be needed if the humanities at this stage are to become the core-subject of the modern curriculum. Here is our great chance to sow the seeds of culture so deep in children that they will withstand the trials of adolescence and fructify in the years ahead. They come to the secondary school full of the first great intellectual enthusiasm and brimming over with curiosity and imagination, living every minute as though it would go on for ever. They come from the junior school ready and willing to express themselves, not yet self-conscious, retaining a large measure of their animal freedom. They come to us, in these last years before adolescence, demanding that we offer them a new world to play in and merely asking that we should explain the new games. For the teacher it is a tremendous opportunity and a demanding situation. What can we offer them?

We can succeed only if we appeal to both mind and senses

in a multiple bill of fare. Thirty years ago Caldwell Cook discovered that Shakespeare provided a feast of such a kind. When Mark Antony addresses the Plebeians in the Forum a glance at the tense faces of the crowd tells us that we are succeeding; when Falstaff seeks recruits outside Mr Justice Shallow's house in Gloucestershire and the children become prostrate with laughter we know we are succeeding; when Shylock rages in front of the Venetian court the curious faces tell us we are succeeding. For these are moments when time and space stand still and they will never be forgotten. Or if it is not drama we can turn to poetry and choral speaking. We can get them to do *Dinas Vawr*, the *Smuggler's Song*, or *Widdicombe Fair*; we can introduce them to ballads such as *Sir Patrick Spens, Lord Randall*, or *Binnorie*; we can be sure that they will like Edward Lear, Lewis Carroll, or W. S. Gilbert; we can turn to the American poet, Vachel Lindsay, and speak *The Congo* and *Daniel Jazz.* And when we have done all this they can sit back and listen while we read to them how the City Slicker instructed Oliver in his first job, or how Huck journeyed down the wide river, the Mississippi. They must have time to learn to speak and to listen to their own incomparable language.

From the ear we must turn in our humanities to the eye and at this point we attach great importance to local studies. We shall teach them to discriminate between the ugly and the beautiful in the study of their own environment. We must take them outside the school and show them the immense variety of their immediate surroundings. Geography and history should be taught at this stage as a single subject. Let a class cooperate in a local survey of the neighbourhood, a survey which will include drawings, maps, diagrams, and models of what they have discovered, and which will be exhibited at the end of the term to their parents and friends. In such a survey we shall combine the work of classroom, art-room, and woodwork shop, and they will learn to use their eyes and hands. By such a method the energies and enthusiasms of every member of a class can be enlisted in the task of jointly discovering something about the world they live in. The careful planning of a visit to a museum can teach them more about their past than they can ever learn from the printed word alone. For to the child of this age the world awaits his personal discovery, whereas it is the purpose of the printed word neatly to package the discoveries of other people. The essence of local studies will be that the children will learn for the first time that the past and the present are linked together; they will learn that this is their inheritance.

Our school (see Diagram 9b, page 223) contains a project room for the use of the children during the years when they will be learning local studies. This is where the projects can be assembled: the information checked in encyclopedias, the maps drawn up and enlarged, the drawings executed under the supervision of the art teacher, whose studio is near by, the models prepared with the assistance of the woodwork teacher, whose shop is also close at hand. The project room will be in a real sense the children's workshop.

The fine arts must complete the cultural core of this curriculum. But what has happened? In 1922 the Board of Education suggested that aesthetic subjects should occupy a minimum of *five* periods a week in the timetable. But in 1938 the Spens Report recorded that 'didacticism is still overweighted in comparison with originating activity', and that 'the activities which are the richest in the creative element have the strongest claim for a place in the curriculum'.(46) We contend that the time is overdue when the fine arts should receive such a place. Although the new-type timetable allots only four periods a week for the fine arts we have already shown that aesthetic appreciation will be an integral part of local studies. When we discuss the school community (see Chapter 9) we shall also show how the fine arts should take their place in the clubs and societies which will occupy the children for one afternoon every week.

The teaching of the fine arts to every child will involve primarily the teaching of aesthetic appreciation. By no means will every child have the ability to make his own music or paint his own picture. Some will have talent as performers but only a few in each generation. We seek to bring an appreciation of the fine arts to the others who will be the majority. In music, for example, we can begin by telling them about the different instruments of the orchestra and getting them to listen to Benjamin Britten's *Young Person's Guide to the Orchestra.* We can explain about music and movement and show them the film of a ballet. We can explain to them on records something about the development of musical forms. And we can do what so many schools already do well – teach them to sing for pleasure. In art we can teach them to appreciate design in all its forms. We shall discard the chronology of art, which has no meaning for young children, and show them the best, the most daring, the most delicate, and the most mature from all the ages. A child can enjoy Breughel as well as Cézanne, Michelangelo as well as Henry Moore, Salisbury Cathedral as well as the Rockefeller Centre in New York, an Attic vase as well as a pressure cooker, or a trireme as well as a modern liner.

Implicit in placing the humanities at the core of the curriculum is the problem of religion and ethics. Piaget's famous inquiry into the origins of moral judgement in children revealed the fact that the child (and indeed the adult) will accept only two moralities: the morality of obedience imposed from above; and the morality of mutual attachment or reciprocity which is the basis of harmonious societies. Between the ages of eleven and thirteen or fourteen children should be taught the Christian religion and as much about the Christian ethical and moral system as they can then understand. A society is very foolish if it does not state clearly to young children the religion upon which its ethical and moral code has been built. At the same time, we foresee that the type of education in the humanities which we are recommending should lead towards the establishment of a morality based upon the experience of mutual obligation.

It is a thoroughly mistaken view to suppose that young children are capable of approaching agnosticism. Neither mentally nor emotionally are they ready for such a view of life. Their happiness at this age whilst they are grappling with the problems of adolescence depends upon the acceptance of an ethical code. In this country the Christian religion is the basis of this ethical code. With the passing of adolescence children very often begin to question the dogma and ethics of Christianity. Towards the end of their school careers, and especially in the sixth form, is the time for such investigation. We think that a majority of parents and teachers, whatever personal beliefs they may hold themselves, would concur with this position.

For we return to our question – How can we develop the personality of the child? Teachers who spend their working lives with children all about them can tell, almost at a glance, the child who has a strong and developing character from the child who has not. The developing personality can be fostered by a curriculum of *activity*; it can be killed by a curriculum of *passivity*. If the humanities are taught in a way which offers to the child a wide variety of experiences in which both mind and senses are equally appealed to, personality will blossom. As a child's personality develops he will be drawn irresistibly into a network of relationships with other children in which slowly he will learn how to 'get along' with other people. If we believe in democracy there is no other way of teaching our children.

The first two years of the curriculum should, therefore, devote approximately half the time to a broad and satisfying study of the humanities. Such a study should be planned as a unity. At the present time a few schools have already been far-sighted enough to plan their curriculum in this way. But the majority treat the curriculum as a trunk full of different subjects not specifically related to each other in any way. If there is no unity there is often little balance and the young mind is introduced all too early to what Ortega y Gasset has called 'the brutality and the stupidity' of the man 'learned in one thing and fundamentally ignorant of all else'. Professionalism and specialization, necessary as they are to contemporary life, can only prove tolerable when they are introduced upon a firm foundation of general education. It is this firm foundation which we hope to achieve in our study of the humanities.

How effectively can the school-leaver communicate?

On 19 December 1959 *Time and Tide*, in its editorial on the Crowther Report, attacked the low standards of British education in these words:

> The symptoms are all around us. After ninety years of compulsory universal schooling we are all in contact with an increasing proportion of youngsters who cannot spell, others who block-letter because they cannot legibly write, telephone-girl trainees who cannot articulate their own language....

On 12 June 1959 Mr K. S. Ferguson, Education and Training Officer for Hoover Ltd, wrote a letter to *The Times Educational Supplement* in which he said:

> Each year we recruit from the ranks of secondary modern schoolboys, aged sixteen to seventeen years, a number of engineering craft apprentices. We submit the candidates to a series of tests which includes an English essay on one of several topics of widespread interest. The average standard of these essays confirms beyond doubt that there is a general and deplorable weakness in the teaching of English in secondary modern schools. Likewise, in my experience of graduate apprentices recruited from a number of universities, there is a regrettable lack of proficiency in the use of English evidenced by the poor standard of many of the reports submitted to me by technical graduates.

And on 22 May 1959, in a joint letter to *The Times Educational Supplement*, the Chairman of the Faculty of English Language and Literature, the Chairman of the Examiners of the Final Honours School of English Language and Literature, and the Chairman of Moderators of the Preliminary Examination in English Language and Literature of Oxford University commented upon the English of candidates at their schools:

> Lack of range showed itself most clearly in pitiably feeble vocabulary. 'Upset' and 'worried' were often the strongest descriptive terms applied to characters of Sophocles, Shakespeare, or Racine in their extremes of passion. Flabby periphrases were substituted for words of strong and definite meaning. From the wide range of

sentence-structures open to writers familiar with English books in any variety, a very few were monotonously chosen.

This editorial and these letters, provoking as they did a storm of controversy, are evidence of a failure to communicate at three different levels. A failure to communicate in the day-to-day use of English; a failure to communicate between the employees of the same industry; and a failure to communicate on the part of the most highly trained of all students of English – the candidates for university Honours.

Turn to our record as students of a foreign language and you will find the same evidence of our failure to communicate. Referring to the standard of French at the Ordinary Level of the General Certificate of Education an experienced teacher poses the question: 'Why are there so many failures after such an expense of energy?' And if the main object of studying a language is to communicate, why does the oral part of the same examination count for as little as 10 out of 220 marks? 'And why', asks the same teacher, 'do we fail so conspicuously, like the Englishman asking for *pâte de dents* in the French chemist's shop?' Why are all but a minority of children unable to communicate their simplest wants in French after four or five years of concentrated study in a secondary school?

'Language', writes another of our correspondents, 'cannot be studied *in vacuo*; its function is to communicate and it must communicate something.' There is no doubt that the really effective teaching of a language, whether it be English or a foreign language, depends very largely on making it an efficient instrument of communication for the child 'at his age'. Children of thirteen are not expected to understand the workings of the Cabinet; it is equally unreasonable to expect them to undertake the analysis of a passage from English literature. Children of fifteen are not expected to accept the responsibilities of an adult; it is unreasonable to expect them to translate a passage from Stendhal's *Le Rouge et le noir* into good English. We might note, *en passant*, that all the countries of Western Europe examine foreign languages orally to a greater extent than we do in this country.

What is the remedy? Take first the fundamental ability to communicate in one's native tongue. This we must achieve, whatever else has to go. We must teach children to 'speak easily and effectively' and to 'listen intelligently'. Speaking should be regarded as an essential part of the study of the English language. Play-reading, recitation, debating, lecturing – all these should be taken really seriously and regarded as of equal importance with the art of writing. There is no reason why we should not devise a series of public examinations in oral English in order to indicate such importance. At the same time we must teach them to listen critically and thus to think intelligently. We cannot ignore the mass media and neither will they. Therefore we must try and develop their taste for the programmes of quality. We must remember that their lives will witness an increase rather than a diminution in the media and we cannot afford not to come to terms with it.

How do we teach them to write well? If we accept the idea that we are teaching them to communicate 'at their age' we must offer the opportunity for writing that is severely practical as well as the more exacting task of creation. After all, for every child who will try at some stage in his life to publish a short story, there will be a thousand who will be faced with the task of making a written application for a job. And the boy who can write an accurate and lively account of a school cricket match which he has actually seen may have learnt already the elements of producing a clear statement of fact for his manager in business. Luckily, the imagination being what it is, there should be no dearth of short-story writers either. For the experience of writing and reading one's original work to one's peers is an experience that young children readily appreciate. Most important of all, however, is that children must learn to take pride in the range and accuracy of their powers of communication. We must show them that they are lucky to have been born into a country with a language and literature of immense variety and strength. Of all the subjects they may have to learn English at least should never be boring.

Turning to foreign languages we reject entirely the old-fashioned idea that there is merit in the study of a language quite irrespective of the results achieved. No respectable Latinist of the nineteenth century would have admitted that there was much value in the study of Latin if it was regularly abandoned at the level of the General Certificate. The whole point of the old classical curriculum was that it led to an understanding, after a whole school-time of study, of the classical world. Such a lengthy study, whether it be of the culture of Greece and Rome or of the culture of France and Russia, remains as the objective for the natural linguist who will carry his study of foreign languages into the sixth form. It is our job to detect such linguistic ability at an early stage in the secondary school and to guide the child forward towards such a course.

For the majority of children, however, the study of a foreign language should deliberately set more limited and therefore more attainable objectives. Many of our correspondents have urged that more weight should be given to oral ability in the language. And many have argued that there is a need for a new type of examination to test these new objectives.

> Why not [says one] a paper which tests the candidate in either letter-writing and general business or commercial French and/or simple questions on such things as currency, communications, industry and/or transcription of a passage of shorthand?

Or, writing on the same problem, another says:

> Speaking generally, it seems a pity that G.C.E. O-level is the only reputable qualification which can be gained by the eleven-plus to fifteen age-group. I think there is need for something else for the 'not-so-academic' child who has achieved something between these ages but who at the moment has little to show for it. The position is of course improving, but much more could be done.

Rejecting, as we do, the concept that a foreign language has great merit as a mind-trainer whatever may be the results achieved, we feel the curriculum should contain one foreign language. There are arguments, both theoretical and practical, which suggest that French should continue to be our first foreign language. From the practical point of view there are likely to be far more qualified teachers of French, both now and in the future, than of any other language. From the theoretical point of view there are a number of arguments. First, as Professor Brogan pointed out in the *Fortnightly Review* in 1942, France like England has a literary culture which can be more easily comprehended through its literature than any other culture except our own. Secondly, he went on to point out that there is value in a country's having an established 'second' language which is taught to children, thus giving them a certain community of interest in another culture. Thirdly, sooner or later these islands will be compelled to relinquish their traditional isolation and move closer to the community of Europe. France, our neighbour in Europe, will be a leading member of this community, and we shall want to be able to communicate with her. Fourthly, we might note that it seems likely that English and French will become the two common languages of post-colonial Africa. For these reasons we should continue the comparatively recent experiment of making French our first foreign language. If the results so far have been disappointing, we must remember that in 1914 there was still no professorial chair of French at either Oxford or Cambridge!

French, therefore, should be taught to the eleven plus to fifteen age-group. It should be examined at the present G.C.E. O-level; it should also be examined at a new and less exclusively literary level which should be readily attainable by a majority of children. During these years we should discover those children who have linguistic ability and prepare them, possibly by a general linguistics course, for learning one or more additional foreign languages – *at pace* – after fifteen.

Communication is a fundamental need for the individual child. There is therefore no case that can be made for teaching him any language which does not enable him to communicate 'at his level' in that language. To achieve this we must offer him a training in the English language that is of extreme practicality as well as of the maximum cultural value. He should leave school quite confident that he can express himself and with some ability to criticize the way his language is used around him in the world. If we fail to give him this much he can rightly accuse us of gross negligence. At the same time we must offer a training in a foreign language that should enable him both to speak to his nearest European neighbour and to understand something of the day-to-day way in which France works. With such equipment the majority will leave school as communicators rather than non-communicators. For those who stay on until the sixth form a good foundation will have been laid.

How skilful is a child when he leaves school?

The gloomier of the prophets during recent years have forecast the collapse of *Homo sapiens* under the sheer efficiency of his machines. For *Homo sapiens* has always been at his best when struggling to do something – for example, when struggling to abolish poverty. When he reaches his objective, so say the prophets, *Homo sapiens*, being essentially a lazy creature, will inevitably just sit back and consume the results of his inventiveness, until in the end he will experience the decay of his mental powers which have brought him in the West to his present incredibly prosperous position in the world. In a child's own words, 'I can enjoy my telly without worrying about science, can't I?' (37) If this is our ultimate fate it will certainly be a tragi-comic end to the story.

Fortunately there are equally strong incentives on the other side to inspire a continuation of the struggle to discover the secrets of the physical world and to diffuse these discoveries throughout a larger proportion of the world's peoples. There are the spectacular fields for discovery like space research or the use of the oceans to provide new sources of energy, food, and water. There are the unspectacular but equally important long-term projects like helping the underdeveloped countries to bypass centuries of history and take their place in the modern world. It seems unlikely that, faced with such challenges, *Homo sapiens* will be content to vegetate, like Mr Ionesco's rhinoceroses, but we would certainly be wise to take all possible precautions against our going out to grass. For in the end even rhinoceroses turn at bay and their only solution to the problem of their diminishing grassland is to fight each other.

There seems to be no reason why children should not enjoy their 'tellys' (since we cannot stop them, we had much better let them get it out of their system), but we want them to worry about science as well. Science will bring a child to grips with the physical world by encouraging his desire to take part in the creative process. He will experience few more immediate satisfactions than those associated with the making of a transistor radio, or breeding hawk moths from caterpillars, or classifying geological specimens. Science will enable a child to be of real help in his own home, perhaps in the kitchen or the garage. Very often today's schoolchild may be in possession at the age of twelve or thirteen of more technical 'know-how' than his parents who suffered education in the pre-scientific age. And science will enable him to enjoy rather more than he would otherwise the making of a living in a scientific world. Should he reach in later life a position of responsibility, it is quite certain that he will need a background of science in taking almost any decision that may come his way.

There are various distinct levels of knowledge which can be acquired and which we loosely describe as science. In the outside world we recognize three levels: the research scientist, the technologist, and the technician. There are only a few research scientists and they spend their time laboriously trying to increase our body of knowledge in various specialized fields. They are usually dedicated people of very high intellectual calibre who may work twelve or sixteen hours a day in their search for truth. In a lifetime of work they may not discover anything which catches the public imagination and may in fact only contribute the sort of knowledge which says 'if you do this nothing happens'! Research scientists are essentially human beings and suffer from human frailties like the rest of us and, although they search for truth professionally, there is no direct evidence that transfer training is any more effective in their case than in anyone else's. You don't need to be a research scientist to appreciate the devastation that can be caused by a nuclear explosion, but you do need at least an acquaintance with the principles of nuclear energy and the effects of radio-activity.

While the research scientist delves into the realms of the unknown the technologist is using and developing known principles. The technologist is highly trained in science and is often involved in what is loosely called research, but should, more precisely, be termed development. He puts theories into practice or rather he directs how theory will be put into practice and the actual 'putting' is done by the technician. The technician is a skilled worker whose skill is in the scientific field.

Now the teaching of science and mathematics in secondary schools has to provide a sound grounding for these different levels of skill. Just as we may now suspect that the doctrine of the enclitic '*de*' was of no help to Lord Milner when faced with the problem of the unification of South Africa, so we may infer that knowledge of non-metallic oxides is not necessarily of general relevance to every schoolchild. What we must do is to devise a curriculum in science and mathematics which is flexible enough to meet different needs. The needs in schools are, more specifically: the need of the science specialist for an academic training in science; the need of the arts specialist for a training in numeracy; the need of the less academically-minded child for a good general acquaintanceship course in science.

Up to G.C.E. O-level, science education for the more able child, in accordance with our feelings about the importance of general education, should satisfy three requirements. First, it should provide a sound basis on which future specialist studies can be developed; second, it should provide a foundation of knowledge sufficiently broad and detailed on which a numeracy course can be built; and third, it must be complete in itself as a balanced picture of the meaning, purpose, methods, and potentialities of science for the sixteen-year-old school-leaver.

There is no doubt about it, the less able child finds science difficult and very tedious. Owing to the paucity of good science teachers and their continual change from job to job, the overcrowding of classes, and the inadequate supply of the right equipment, the less able child is soon convinced that science is for eggheads only and is no concern of his, 'thank goodness'. Yet from this vast source of manpower we want to obtain some of our technicians.

To sum up the position as far as G.C.E. O-level, we find that mathematics courses tend to be rather too complete without enough leads into sixth-form work, although this is provided by courses following additional mathematics at O-level. Science courses, on the other hand, require, for the most part, a sixth-form course to make sense of middle-school teaching. In the case of the less able child interest, curiosity, enthusiasm, and enjoyment must be derived from a study of mathematics and science, but an acquaintanceship course must be within the scope of the child.

In the sixth form we shall be training the research scientists and the technologists in their specialist subjects and they will join with the arts specialists to study the 'Development of Scientific Thought'. The arts specialists will complete their scientific culture with either mathematics or statistics. We shall be giving the less able sixth-former a choice of subjects which will include mathematics and science. The full details of the courses we propose and the time to be spent on them are discussed in Chapter 6.

Looking a little more closely into the study of the physical world we find that in schools this study is usually divided into a number of subjects: mathematics, physics, chemistry, and biology. Sometimes these subjects are further divided – e.g. organic, inorganic, and physical chemistry; pure and applied mathematics; botany and zoology – and sometimes combined, e.g. general science. Combinations tend to take place in the early years of a school science course and divisions at a later stage. It is most important from the child's point of view that, where coherence between the individual subjects comprising the group exists, it should be emphasized.

> Mathematics has been described as the 'Queen and Servant of the sciences'. It is easy and natural for mathematics to assume the first of these roles and to preserve a regal distance between herself and her subjects. But there is also a dignity of labour, and mathematics loses nothing and gains much from helping the other sciences.(56)

It is this help as the tool and language of science that can give the child confidence in the subject. As a tool the relevant mathematics must be available when it is required. Sometimes the scientist wants to use some topics in mathematics before his mathematical colleague thinks it proper. This is a difficult problem to solve, but it is important for the teachers concerned to solve it and come to a useful compromise so that the child does not wallow in unnecessary difficulties. It has been suggested that the syllabuses of work in geography, mathematics, and science should be exhibited in parallel columns to be studied by the teachers concerned to see what topics they have in common, when they should be taught, and what aspects of each common topic should be taught by whom.

To take an example, towards the end of an O-level course in geometry we are taught that 'The ratio of the areas of similar figures is that of the squares on the corresponding sides and that the ratio of the volumes of similar solids is that of the cubes on the corresponding sides'. In biology this principle can be used to explain the shape of birds, for if the dimensions of a small bird were doubled then the area of the wings would only be four times as great and would have to support a weight eight times as large. Compare, for example, the shape of a sparrow and a seagull. Or again in chemistry we can explain why a powdered solid dissolves more readily than the same weight in a lump because if we have 512 grains of powder $\frac{1}{512}$ of the original weight then the surface area will be increased eight times. Or to take an example in physics, one pound of hailstones $\frac{1}{8}$ in. in diameter dropped from 1,000 feet will bounce lightly off your umbrella, but in the form of a single large stone of approximately 4 in. diameter it would go straight through a car roof, the resistance of the fall being proportional to the surface area, which decreases the total resistance experienced by the large stone to $\frac{1}{32}$ of the total resistance experienced by the small stones. The principle can even be used to explain why children can walk barefoot on a pebbly beach in more comfort than their parents.

When relationships of this sort arise naturally and readily between the sciences they should be used to help the child gain a more coherent picture of the physical world.

Some mathematics is taught in the primary stage and, as this is the beginning of ten years' study for every child and considerably more for some children, it is important that

> no new process should be taught until the pupil is ready for it (i.e., has the mental ability to learn it), the basic skills are established, and until the process has meaning for him as the result of experience that shows him its social value.[57]

The timing of the introduction of new topics in mathematics is most important; long periods spent using drill methods for solving simultaneous equations by the very young, who are following an algebraic routine without knowing what they are doing or why, is a degradation of mathematics. Simultaneous equations can be taught quite shortly, and can be clearly understood two years after leaving the primary school. The valuable time thus saved could be spent perhaps in getting some idea of the spatial aspects of mathematics, really getting to grips with the simpler solids, making models and taking measurements of them.

Mathematics, then, is the first 'science' that the child meets and it is used as a basis of science aptitude on selection at the 11-plus by most authorities. Mathematics is also included in the curriculum in its own right because it is the language of orderliness and orderly thinking, because it is part of our culture, and because it can give genuine pleasure.

Science appears on the curriculum for the first time in secondary schools. Children come to their first science classes with a sense of expectancy. They have considerable interest in and sometimes knowledge of science derived from films, magazines, books, hobbies, and television, and they want to develop it. Because of this sense of expectancy, this feeling that science will help them in an immediate and practical way to understand the world, the organization of science teaching is of great importance. Enthusiasm not requited will quickly die. Science is the subject of the 'here and now' to young children and nobody will feel more quickly than they the utter futility of learning by rote masses of semi-useless facts. To them there is a unity about the world, and the compartmentalization of science will seem essentially unreal and unnecessary. And of course if five or six different people teach them science in the course of a single year because our affluent society cannot afford to pay enough to make science teaching an attractive career, there is very little chance that the children's initial enthusiasm will be retained.

> They had come from the primary school with a real curiosity about the world and their place in it. By the time I stood before them, this curiosity was almost dead.[37]

By thirteen the children in this school had had science effectively killed for them.

Of great importance in the field of scientific education in this country are the Science Masters' Association and the Association of Women Science Teachers. Early in 1961 the two associations issued a policy statement called *Science and Education*, mainly concerning grammar schools. This statement we wish to discuss in some detail. The general recommendations of the statement are as follows:

> We maintain that science should be a 'core' subject in grammar schools in the same way as, for example, English and mathematics are at present and as Classics used to be. To achieve this we recommend that
>
> 1. *All* pupils should follow a balanced course of science subjects up to the end of the fifth-form year. Although science in the widest sense may be concerned with all human experience, the school science must be more restricted in scope. It should lie within the range of the so-called 'natural sciences', each of which is concerned

with a limited aspect of human experience. It is essential that pupils should be helped to appreciate the wide range of science as a whole, but their formal course should consist mainly of work involving the sciences of biology, chemistry, and physics, with some astronomy and geology if possible, even if geology is studied as part of a geography course. The depth to which such a course is studied should depend more on the abilities of the pupils than on the subjects in which they intend to specialize. There should, in fact, be no division into science specialists and arts specialists until beyond this level, so that specialization in arts or science, or even a combination of the two, may be available to all pupils of the necessary ability when they enter the sixth form.

2. Science should be studied by *all* pupils in the sixth form. We have in mind, not the specialist courses in a few sciences leading to the advanced level and scholarship examinations, but a broader course which should enable pupils to attain the scientific literacy which the Crowther Report calls 'numeracy', though much more than numerical issues are involved.

3. Subject specialization should be retained in the sixth form, thus continuing a long-established tradition in this country, but advanced-level syllabuses should be reduced as regards the detailed factual content which has become so great in some of them. Such a reduction should release time for the broader course proposed in Recommendation 2.[(50)]

Whilst we endorse the second recommendation, we do not agree with the policy statement as a whole. We do not think that education should be developed on rigid lines round any core subject with its limited aspect of human experience, but rather that education should have as its primary aim the development of the personality of the child. Whilst we agree that science should be taught to all pupils during their first four or five years, we feel that the introduction of science culture from which the other studies would derive their inspiration would burden the sciences with difficulties which they would be unable to resolve. Whilst we agree that the amount of specialization at present undertaken by the science sixth is too great, we doubt whether the arts syllabuses are in fact overburdened factually. Our inquiries have revealed that historians, linguists, and English specialists feel the need for a changed outlook and new content rather than a reduction in the quantity of the syllabus.

Our proposals for the amount of time to be devoted to science in the middle-school curriculum are illustrated in the new-type curriculum (Diagram 2, page 98). We feel that any proposals, to be realistic, must take into account the availability of science teachers. In an appendix to their policy statement the S.M.A. and the A.W.S.T. reveal that their proposals would require about twice as many teachers of science in the middle school as are needed at the moment. Yet there is already a critical shortage. In Table 2 we have compared the number of science periods which are taught at present with the number proposed under the S.M.A./A.W.S.T. statement and with the new-type curriculum.

Table 2 *Time allocated to Science and Mathematics (unit: periods per week)*

	'Old-type' Curriculum		*S.M.A. Scheme*		*'New-type' Curriculum*	
	Science	*Maths*	*Science*	*Maths*	*Science*	*Maths*
1st year	4	6	6	5	3	5
2nd year	4	6	6	5	3	5
3rd year	4	6	9	4	6	5
4th year	4	6	9*	4	6	5
5th year	4	6	9*	4	6	5
Totals	20	30	39	22	24	25

* S.M.A. consider this a minimum and say that it should be 12 for all but the best pupils.

Our conclusion is that the S.M.A./A.W.S.T. policy statement is unworkable. The S.M.A. and the A.W.S.T. have done much valuable work for the teaching of science in schools, but this policy statement is not the answer to the problem. It was no doubt produced at a time when concern about science teaching had become something of a national neurosis in Britain. But its recommendations are neither cultural nor realistic.

In the new-type curriculum (Diagram 2, page 98) the proposals for scientific education have one novel feature. We consider that science, being a mature pursuit, is of the greatest value when taught to older children. There is a good deal of discussion nowadays about whether or not to 'introduce science' into the primary school. This is to tackle the problem at the wrong end. What the primary schools have long been doing in nature study is the right kind of approach and all our thought should be devoted to the really vital problem of ensuring that children leave school sufficiently numerate to take their place in a scientific world. The new-type curriculum therefore is designed to provide a scientific education which satisfies three needs:

1. It provides a stimulating course for the child of eleven to thirteen with the aim of building up the child's natural enthusiasm and curiosity;
2. It provides a solid grounding for the child of thirteen to fifteen with the aim of ensuring that no child leaves school without a general scientific background;
3. It provides a sixth-form education in which the non-science specialist – about fifty per cent of all sixth-formers – is able to continue with the study of coherence subjects and devote about six periods a week to the scientific field.

Later in this book there is a discussion of sixth-form education (see Chapter 6); for the moment we will consider the science that should be taught in the middle school.

Most children, we consider, should be taking a general science course, with the exception of the very bright grammar-school child who may be taking separate subjects. The syllabus for general science, as laid down by the Science Masters' Association, is very good. It is a pity that the examinations that test this course should be so inadequate that cramming is very easy. The new-type timetable proposals, which are based on a forty-week year, give 720 science periods in a four-year course, or 960 science periods in a five-year course. The period requirements for the general science course are 519 periods for the 'ordinary course' and 690 periods for the 'extended course'. There is, therefore, plenty of time available, and individual children taking physics, chemistry, and biology as separate subjects at G.C.E. O-level will also have sufficient time for their studies.

The general science course should be taught by one man and not divided up at this stage into three different subjects with three different teachers. There is a reason for this. We envisage that a trained teacher will in future hold Part 1 of the Degree in Education (see Chapter 10); and this will be an entirely adequate qualification for teaching general science. Specialist physicists, chemists, and biologists will be needed to reduce drastically the size of the sets in the science sixths and also to teach the coherence subjects, like 'The Development of Scientific Thought', to the sixth form as a whole. We think that the scientific element in the Degree in Education should aim specifically at equipping future teachers with the special qualities that will be needed to teach the general science course. For instance, if the boredom of children with science at the early age of thirteen is to be avoided it is quite clear that the Degree in Education must be very much concerned with the question of how to present the subject of general science to young children as well as with equipping the teacher with the necessary philosophical background. Our investigations have shown that the scientific specialist is not by any means the best teacher of science to young children, and we feel that here is a field very apposite to the Degree in Education.

In the middle school, therefore, the new type curriculum will provide at every stage an expanding course in mathematics and science closely linked to each other and to kindred subjects such as geography. From the age of eleven a child will experience an introduction to the physical world which will grow in depth as he matures in his outlook and which will lead him in the sixth form into the study of the basic nature and the aims of science. By treating science as a mature subject we shall avoid the boredom that can come to young children when faced with such complex problems. It is this boredom which so often leads in adult life to the not uncommon outlook of 'anti-science'. By this method of slowly expanding the content of scientific education, instead of just increasing the amount of time devoted to science in all years, we seek to retain the child's initial interest and enthusiasm.

For the less academically minded child, however, it will be necessary to provide the alternative of more practical education. In the middle school a proportion of the time he would otherwise spend on science, and possibly the whole of the time that he would spend on French, should go to training in practical skills like woodwork, metalwork, or other crafts. There is no reason why his timetable should not be adjusted to include these skills while retaining the other subjects in the curriculum. For the more academically minded child, pursuing the full curriculum, this practical training will take place on the weekly afternoon devoted to clubs and societies. This we shall discuss more fully when we talk about the school community (see Chapter 9).

By what criterion shall we judge our standards of numeracy in the future? We should surely expect people to understand the fundamentals of a scientific world so that most people will have more than a vague idea of the progress and problems of technology. We should hope that people will know enough of practical science to make use of the aids to more civilized living that will come their way. We would like to think that, in casting their democratic vote on great issues, people will at any rate be acquainted with the scientific background of these issues. But if none of these, then perhaps we may be spared such grosser breaches of truth as that of the journalist who wrote, when describing an air accident in the stratosphere 'and then the escape hatch blew off and the rarefied air rushed in'!

The integration of science into our traditional culture is one of the most important tasks of the immediate future. Our grammar schools have long provided excellent training for the future specialist scientist. This they must continue to do. The new task which awaits all types of secondary schools is to make a much wider range of people scientifically minded. We need many more people in all walks of life who are well acquainted with the fundamentals of science and who can relate this knowledge to their own jobs and to the modern world. This is the aim of our proposals.

Is the present system of physical education satisfactory? A weekly article in *The Times Educational Supplement* under the title of '*In Corpore Sano*' gives the reader an idea of the range of physical activities undertaken by today's schoolchildren. It is an impressive tribute to the courage and energy of children and the skill and enthusiasm of the men and women who plan these activities. What is so encouraging is that these activities seem to combine an excellent training in the building of physique and the development of children's characters while preserving their freedom of choice and self-expression. True, our chess enthusiasts do not, like the Russians, undergo an arduous course of physical training in preparation for the championships, but Victor Sylvester has made no secret of the fact that he has done regular physical training during his long career as a dancing master. What the reader may not always realize is that behind all these excellent activities lies the groundwork of physical education in schools.

The work of the schools depends upon intelligent organization and good buildings and equipment. The organization must contend with the usual problem of the timetable. P.E. should be integrated into the timetable and not merely filled in on the plan after other demands have been satisfied. It is not the poor relation in the curriculum, certainly not to the child, who should gain real enjoyment and relaxation during this period, and it should not be so considered by the staff. In view of the urbanization of our society, with its vast increase in sedentary work, physical education is a great deal more important today than ever before. If schools do not carry out this education really effectively, tomorrow's citizens may well find themselves unable to stand up to the pressures of urban society. Therefore, in view of its importance in the curriculum, the time is long past when the P.E. specialist could be regarded as a kind of second-class teacher in the staff-room. P.E. takes its place in the curriculum as a fully equal partner in the whole complex business of educating children. The buildings should be designed to afford the greatest amount of flexibility. A school gymnasium, for example, may be used at one time or another for almost every school activity: assembly hall, stage, examination-room, net-ball and basketball court, fencing salle, boxing-ring, judo arena, circuit-training area, table-tennis room, and of course the many daily periods of physical training. In it must be stored a variety of equipment for different sports and different ages; it is no use expecting a boy of eleven to handle a medicine ball that is suit-able for a boy of fifteen. The gymnasium must also contain proper changing-rooms, washrooms, and showers, for it is pointless to preach the need for personal hygiene while deny-ing the child the means to carry it out. Sound building and sound planning are the prerequisites of good physical educa-tion.

In 1957 the Ministry of Education published a magnificent book on physical education called *Moving and Growing.*[42] Although written for the primary school this book, embodying really up-to-date thinking and experience, has had a profound effect on the teaching of P.E. in all schools. P.E. periods in the gymnasium should have five major aims:

1. Enjoyable relaxation and exercise, and the development of muscular control;
2. Posture and physique, which will include grace, carriage, and balance;
3. Fitness, hardness, and strength;
4. Skills and techniques, for gymnastics, for athletics and other games;
5. Character training.

What was at one time, and not so very long ago, a matter of 'physical jerks', has now given place to a deliberate, co-ordinated programme for developing the growing body of the child towards its optimum efficiency in everyday life as an adult.

This is a very different idea from just exercising children in the time available in the curriculum once everything else has had its cut. Anyone who has visited a school on an Open Day and witnessed a display of gymnastics and physical education should delight at the progress which schools have made since his own childhood. Nor should the work which is done in remedial classes for the physically handicapped be forgotten. It is our job to ensure that schools do all that they can to give children the best possible physical equipment for life.

A school must have a policy for games, which is best laid down by the head advised by a games committee of teachers and children. This policy should deal with the question of compulsory and voluntary games and with the question of major and minor games. Because the successful teaching of games is largely a matter of enthusiasm on the part of the teachers, the most modest of men is likely to become wildly irrational when fighting for the services of a particular child or the provision of extra time for his particular game. In the course of the scramble the needs of the child who is only an average games player are likely to be forgotten. A school games policy must of course be based upon the numbers of games places available at any given time in each sport. There are strong arguments, which we endorse, for making a team-game compulsory for all boys, at any rate, during their years in the middle school (eleven to fifteen). Soccer, rugger, hockey, cricket, rowing, and athletics are such team-games. These games will not appeal to every boy, but all of them provide him with excellent exercise (cricket after all takes place in nets as well as on the field). They also offer very good opportunities for teaching boys how to cooperate with one another and how to exercise a type of leadership very different in kind from the *Führerprinzip*. The minor games, like tennis, squash, fives, fencing, and various forms of projecting missiles at targets, should be provided for boys on a voluntary basis. A school games policy must be judged not only by the standard of expertise reached by the first eleven or by the first fifteen, but also by the enjoyment and relaxation provided for every boy in the school.

Organized games playing in girls' schools has been much maligned as purposelessly aping the boys' tradition and either producing hearty hockey players or a tight-skirted, unenthusiastic, unskilled rabble. Team games have, in moderation, as much to teach girls as they have boys and should form part of the compulsory curriculum. To the age of thirteen or fourteen the majority of girls are likely to be keen. After this age many girls do not take kindly to hockey, lacrosse, or netball; there should then be a wider scope for individual activities such as tennis, athletics, swimming, archery, or dancing. In order to carry out a programme of this sort adequate staffing is a first essential. Girls' schools are provided with a greater proportion of P.E. specialists than boys' and in many schools the equipment provided is generous. But too often the P.E. department is a very fluid one, consisting of young teachers and part-timers. The resultant lack of continuity in teaching has a serious effect on the girls' enthusiasm and the standard of skills achieved.

The provision of a swimming-bath in a school is an expensive matter. In a big school, say a comprehensive school for 2,000 children, the estimates will provide for five or six gymnasia. A swimming-bath costs about £25,000 and is roughly the equivalent of the expenditure on two gymnasia. In these big schools it is possible to put in a bath by cutting down on the number of gymnasia and alternating orthodox P.E. periods with swimming periods. Many smaller schools have regular periods allocated to them during the school week in public baths. Our unplanned towns of the nineteenth century all too often neglected to put in public swimming-baths and it is significant that only Cardiff has a bath which is adequately equipped for Olympic swimming in the British Isles. We place a high emphasis on the value of teaching children to swim.

There is a strong case against boxing for older and stronger boys, although it has much to commend it for smaller boys. Medical evidence has shown that it is quite possible for a boy who weighs ten stone or more to inflict serious injury in the boxing-ring.

One further point about the organization of physical education. There is very little time available in the curriculum. It is obviously a waste to use a proportion of this time at the beginning and end of term on the time-honoured practice of 'weighing and measuring' and writing reports. To write reports on 500 children whom he takes for one period a week is an uneconomical use of a specialist's skill. Far better that he should be getting on with the job in hand.

Associated with physical education is the question of personal hygiene. Time must be found for instruction in personal hygiene and kindred topics. First Aid should certainly be taught to every child while he is at school. Perhaps there will be opportunities for instruction in First Aid in one of the clubs which meet in the afternoons (see Chapter 9). If not we should surely deal with it within the ordinary classroom curriculum. A concerted campaign twenty years ago to teach schoolchildren the 'Rule of the Road' has resulted in a remarkable reduction in the annual toll of accidents. We wonder if a campaign to teach elementary First Aid to all children would not have similar results in the numbers who frequent doctors' surgeries with minor injuries?

Extra P.E. should not be used as the main vehicle of punishment in a school. We do not want to give children the impression that physical education is something which they ought to dislike. There are many more effective ways of punishing children in a social context which will teach them that they have acted against the spirit of their own society. P.E., we feel strongly, should be something they enjoy.

Although discovered by the Greeks, physical education is a newcomer to the curriculum of English schools. Its late appearance in the curriculum has meant that the older men now teaching P.E. in schools have very often had only a short course of emergency-type training like that provided immediately after the war for all teachers. Before the war men who required a full-time course in physical education had to go abroad, probably to Scandinavia, to get a training. The Ministry of Education has recently suggested that men who teach P.E. should hold a degree in order that they may turn over to the academic side later on. This, we consider, would not produce satisfactory results, because academic teaching to children is better done if started young. However, the Degree in Education (see Chapter 10) should provide the right qualification for the P.E. specialist and should enable him, provided the staffing ratio of P.E. teachers is increased, to take academic work in addition to directing physical education.

The ancient world respected the human body. Every Greek shrine or city had its stadium where the games were held. Human physique provided the subject-matter for great art. It was not until the Renaissance that a similar concern for the human body was displayed by European civilization. From this concern has sprung the growth of medical science, which is the greatest boon of modern times. Physical education is essential for every child. Both the physical education provided for by periods in the school timetable and the games that go on outside are necessary to the physical development of the child. Physical education can also help him to develop his character generally. For many children the games that they play will provide the happiest moments of their school career. For those who leave school at fifteen and for those whose school is not yet adequately equipped with playing-fields, we must campaign vigorously for more and better public provision. Our cities need playing-fields, athletics tracks, and swimming-baths; they are not luxuries but essentials for the young. Here is something that we can do for children which may play a considerable part in ensuring their future health and stability.

In this chapter we have discussed the new-type curriculum with particular reference to the early years in the secondary school. From eleven to thirteen the curriculum will devote over half the time to the humanities, the arts, and the English language. These subjects will be studied together in much the same way as they were during the later years at the primary school. In the 'Plan for the Secondary School' (Diagrams 9a and b, page 223) the work will take place in the junior school sited on its own side of the building and proximate to the

Diagram 2 *'New-Type' Curriculum*

PERIODS				
1				
2				
3		FRENCH	FRENCH	
4				
5				
6				
7	COMMUNICATION			
8		ENGLISH	ENGLISH Language and Literature	
9				2½ SPECIALIST SUBJECTS
10				
11		ENGLISH CULTURE	CURRENT AFFAIRS	
12				
13				
14		NARRATIVE HISTORY	HISTORY	
15				
16	HUMANITIES			
17		LOCAL STUDIES	GEOGRAPHY	
18				
19				
20		RELIGION *and* ETHICS	GENERAL SCIENCE *or* PHYSICS CHEMISTRY *and/or* BIOLOGY	1½ COHERENCE SUBJECTS *Science* 1. The Development of Scientific Thought 2. English and History 3. Modern Language *Arts* 1. The Development of Scientific Thought 2. English *or* History *or* Modern Language 3. Mathematics *or* Statistics
21				
22				
23		GENERAL SCIENCE		
24				
25				
26	NUMERACY			
27		MATHEMATICS	MATHEMATICS	
28				
29				
30				CURRENT AFFAIRS
31		MUSIC	RELIGION *and* ETHICS	
32	ARTS			COMPARATIVE RELIGION
33		ART	MUSIC *or* ART	
34				MUSIC *or* ART
35		PHYSICAL EDUCATION	PHYSICAL EDUCATION	PHYSICAL EDUC.

AGE 11+ 12+ 13+ 14+ 15+ 16+ 17+

rooms for crafts, art, and music. It is intended that these first two years in the secondary school should provide the child with an educational experience that is largely self-contained.

We have also discussed the place of science and mathematics in the 'new-type' curriculum during the period from eleven to fifteen – that is prior to entry into the sixth form. Science and mathematics will be studied as mutually supporting subjects which provide the child with his introduction to the physical world. We have rejected the view that the curriculum should devote substantially more time than at present to the study of these subjects. Instead we have proposed that science should be treated as one of the expanding subjects. It is a mature discipline that should play an increasing part in the child's education until the time when he enters the sixth form and becomes capable of attaining numeracy.

Finally we have stressed the importance of a planned programme of physical education for every child.

CHAPTER 5

A Curriculum to Suit the Needs of the Child: The Needs from Above

To what extent can we prepare the child, so shortly to become a young adult, for the demands which society will make upon him? There should be new emphasis in the curriculum for the child of thirteen to fourteen designed to guide him forward from his pre-adolescent world towards the world of his maturity. Already at thirteen years of age he has become the potential school-leaver of two or three years later. We must cater as best we can for those whose education will end at the statutory school-leaving age. At the same time we must provide for those who will stay on and go into the sixth form. This second stage of the secondary curriculum can neither be regarded as a preparation exclusively for the teenage world outside the school nor for the sixth form within the school. It must be planned as an educational experience that is complete within itself whilst providing a broad and satisfying background for the child's future. At the same time the curriculum must provide a continuity with all that has gone before. Therefore our discussion will concern not only the three questions about the needs of the child which have not yet been answered but also a further amplification of the four questions we have considered in Chapter 4.

Is our education an adequate preparation for becoming a good citizen?

Unlike the Americans we have always taken democracy for granted. Indeed, it is fashionable in some circles to sneer at the very considerable attempts which the Americans make through their educational system to teach children about democracy. Responsible self-government, we are inclined to assume, is something which just grows naturally; not a precious seed which has to be carefully planted in our midst. Unfortunately there is no justification for this assumption whatsoever. Every day we are reminded that unless people understand what democracy means democracy itself will perish – and possibly far sooner than we can imagine. We quote from the *Observer* of 9 July 1961:

> Speaking to the annual conference of the Mineworkers, Mr Hill [Chairman of the T.U.C.] advised trade unionists not to lose too much sleep over the E.T.U. case: ballot rigging had been going on since 'time immemorial'.

We quote from the *Sunday Telegraph* of the same date:

> Thousands of passengers may be operating a rail-ticket fraud on London's Underground and suburban train services ... some of the British Transport Commission's gigantic losses are caused by fraudulent travel.

Clearly neither the Chairman of the T.U.C. nor the thousands of passengers who daily cheat themselves on the railways have much conception of how a democratic society works.

Because democracy is the most complex system of government yet devised by man it is absolutely essential that children should understand its fundamental workings. We have already indicated that a curriculum that is merely a collection of different 'subjects' taught to a syllabus conceived primarily as a 'subject syllabus' is inadequate for such an understanding. For only the very intelligent child is capable of building the mental bridges necessary to bring these subjects into relation with each other. For the majority the subjects remain unrelated to each other and usually unrelated to their world of contemporary events. The picture of the world that is built up in their minds becomes inevitably fragmented and meaningless. Instead of receiving an education that poses clearly and dynamically the major issues of their society, they leave school with a knowledge of society that appears to them largely irrelevant at the time. They therefore lose little time in jettisoning such knowledge for the far more interesting experience provided by 'life'. As a teenage club member recently put it:

> 'You don't learn nothin' at school, anything. They just "tell" you. Do things. Learn dates. Nobody takes an interest in you, y'know, find out what you really could do. I hated school.' (36)

From thirteen to fifteen or sixteen we begin to pose to the child the questions about society and the contemporary world which we regard as an essential training for citizenship. These questions will be discussed during periods on history, geography, and current affairs; there is no doubt that they will also arise during periods devoted to the study of religion and ethics. We seek to impose no answers, but we do not seek to be quite impartial. For we want above all to awaken interest and enthusiasm rather than merely put forward a cold analysis which will make little impact. We shall stick quite closely to the practical because even at this age the young mind has little capacity for the essentially grown-up practice of intellectual criticism. For example, if we are discussing social welfare, much more will be gained by getting the children themselves to draw up their plans for a new town than by a detailed analysis of the way in which the Ministry of Health carries out its functions. Or, if we are discussing race relations, we should hold a debate on the motion 'That this house would pass immigration laws' rather than discuss the situation in Central Africa. Very often at the end of such a debate when enthusiasm has been aroused we can teach best by correcting the inaccuracies of the speakers. By these methods we shall indicate to them that these questions, still largely outside their experience, are nevertheless questions of importance.

But from the age of thirteen onwards there is a difficulty. Inevitably a great deal of time in the curriculum must be devoted to the examinable subjects and we have already indicated that democracy does not lend itself to academic examination. Many schools, however, devote a term of the history syllabus in the third or fourth year to the teaching of citizenship, and children respond eagerly to such a course. Others prepare children to take a paper on the British Constitution at G.C.E. O-level and this also seems to have a wide appeal at this age.

In the middle school a good deal depends upon the teaching of history. A lengthy correspondence from history teachers in *The Times Educational Supplement* early in 1960 revealed two distinct viewpoints. On the one hand there were those, teaching mostly the more intelligent children, who took their stand on the fact that they were 'not holding a mirror up to the modern world but, with the past as material, were grinding an objective lens for some of its inhabitants'.[64] On the other hand there were those, usually working with the less intelligent children, who contended that their job was 'to take the present out of a vacuum and to situate it fairly and squarely in the context of past events which have led up to it'.[64] During the course of the correspondence neither side would budge one iota!

History, like science, is a mature study and should certainly be treated as one of the expanding subjects in the curriculum. The new-type curriculum will ensure that a good deal of history, both in 'The Development of Scientific Thought' and in straight history courses, will be taught to sixth-formers. Here we feel is the opportunity for the 'grinders of the objective lens' school of historians. For the child who will leave school before the sixth form we feel that emphasis must be placed, as Mr John Sharp suggested, upon an understanding of the modern world. If we must choose between the Wars of the Roses and the Russian Revolution we shall choose the Russian Revolution; if we must choose between the Enclosure Movement and the first Industrial Revolution we shall choose the first Industrial Revolution; and so on. We shall try to teach children the history whose consequences can still be seen in contemporary society.

Most fifteen-year-olds need plenty of time in school and the best teaching in order to become really literate in their own tongue: not just enough to pass easy examinations, but sufficient to give them a lively pleasure in reading, speaking, and writing. They need to be introduced to the arts and given opportunity to practise them. These are not flowers, but roots of education.[44]

Crowther noticed that at about the age of fourteen, and more especially in boys' schools, 'the English subjects tend to go to the wall'. Very often history and geography become alternatives, art and music cease to be compulsory, and English itself becomes the poor relation to languages and science. At an age when children can begin to take pride in the study and practice of their own culture they are denied the opportunity to do so. The reason why this happens is that under the existing curriculum children must choose additional (usually referred to as 'optional') subjects at the early age of thirteen or fourteen. These additional subjects are either the extension of science to include separate courses in physics, chemistry, and biology, or a second foreign language. The choice once made not only transfers an extra six or eight weekly periods to the new subject(s) but also commits the child to a particular sixth form later on. In practice few children are mature enough to know at this age what particular group of subjects will form their main interest at a later time. The choice is therefore made for them by their teachers. The teachers must go upon their performance so far in the elementary stages of the subject which is not always the most accurate predictor of later progress. Our proposals for the teaching of general science, *one* foreign language, and the ending of compulsory Latin are designed to eliminate – for the majority – the necessity for such a choice (see Chapter 4). Our later proposals for the sixth-form curriculum are designed to prevent sixth-form specialization casting its shadow upon the middle-school years. The 'ABC' proposals recently put forward by some headmasters have the same object in view (see page 139).

The time saved should go to the vital task of helping fourteen- and fifteen-year-olds 'to become really literate in their own tongue'. The new-type curriculum allots five weekly periods to the study of English language and English literature. However much the exigencies of particular schools and particular examinations may affect the curriculum, these five periods, or roughly one period per day of English, must not be tampered with. They are just as important to the 'A'-stream child as to the 'c'-stream child. They are of increasing importance in schools which contain a large proportion of first-generation secondary-school children who come so often from homes where books are not read and literary interests not cultivated. If the schools do not go all out for literacy nobody else can or will.

What sort of approach should be made to the teaching of English to fourteen- or fifteen-year-olds? In a language so rich and complex as our own one man's meat will not necessarily be another's. The child must have variety. A teacher who can get a class of children to *enjoy* their English periods with him, by whatever methods, achieves his aim. In the teaching of English the work in all its aspects – including the necessary examinations – should be a synthesis of the interests of the children stimulated and directed by the knowledge and enthusiasm of the teacher. Children's interests, we know, are spontaneous, often ephemeral, and deeply felt. They will respond to an equally deep and intensely felt knowledge of the subject on the part of the teacher.

Ideally, the first-rate teacher of English should retain a little radicalism all his life. Of the early Empson it was said in literary circles: 'We gather he isn't quite sound on Shelley.' To be 'sound' as a teacher of English is almost certainly to be dull and so to bore children. Once children are bored no amount of exhortation and personal encouragement will persuade them to devour the books of a favourite author or to write for pleasure their own poetry or prose. They will go through the motions of formal set-work; they will, no doubt, pass the English language paper of the G.C.E.; but real literacy with its lifelong command and appreciation of their own language will elude them.

Almost everything therefore depends upon the teacher. But he need not quail because he has one great ally – the English language itself. Inevitably at the start of his career he will not be so well equipped as he might be. He must exhort little and encourage much, remembering that if he can only provide the right material for the children to work on the books themselves will do the job. As time goes on, provided he takes all his opportunities to extend his range, he will acquire an expertise that will inevitably communicate itself to children. The school must allow him freedom to experiment and it must provide a library fit for such a task.

English is not an ordered body of knowledge that can be acquired in a stated period of time like a syllabus in science. Few of us can remember more than a smattering of the books and poems which we studied at school. But there are one or two rules which the teacher should follow when he grapples with the partly literate child. Firstly he must remember that it is the child's language as much as it is his own, and if he selects books which do not kindle the imagination and challenge the mind, however much he may enjoy reading these books himself, they will make no impression upon the child. It is the teacher's job to search tirelessly until he lights upon literature that children can enjoy at their own particular age. Secondly, there is the grammar of the language. Unless children are taught where they go wrong grammatically and why it is wrong, they may write with real feeling and enthusiasm but make no progress. Teachers of all subjects must insist firmly upon English grammar and syntax. And thirdly, and most easily from the teacher's point of view, there should be great scope for the free expression of childish imagination unfettered by the demands of examinations and text-books. How often are such admirable ideas as form magazines, form plays, or form debates suppressed by otherwise intelligent teachers in favour of the more comfortable and ordered routine of an English syllabus. And yet it is precisely with work of this kind, work carried out under conditions of complete imaginative freedom, that many children mature and develop their control of language.

Effective communication is the basis of our civilization. Without any doubt the English language is destined to be one of the five or six great languages of the future as it is today one of the major world languages. It is the greatest cultural asset possessed by every English man and woman. It is folly if we do not trade upon this asset in educating our children.

'The elementary stages of two foreign languages do not

double the intellectual value of one.' [44] There is little of culture in the early stages of learning a new language. Athough a child gains some useful linguistic discipline in these early stages there is no compelling reason why such discipline should be gained at the expense of studying two languages at the age of thirteen or fourteen and at the cost of using nearly a third of the curriculum. The new-type curriculum allows a child to carry through the study of *one* foreign language, usually French, to a point where he begins to gain from the rich influence of another culture. There is no rationale behind the present practice of starting a second foreign language before the child has got much farther towards the mastery of a first language and the mastery of his native tongue. The able linguist will in fact pick up a second foreign language at far greater speed in the sixth form when he will be able to benefit from his previous experience in learning *one* language to some depth. There will be a few children, the high-fliers, destined from an early age to the mastery of several foreign languages. For the majority the study of *one* foreign language, within the broad curriculum, will be far more satisfactory. There is also a case, we believe, for experimentation in a course of general linguistics in order to introduce children to problems of communication. Those of our correspondents who have suggested such a course have often reported favourably on the satisfactory results achieved in such a course at the expenditure of no more than two or three weekly periods of teaching.

What can children be expected to know after four or five years of study in a foreign language? Let us endorse the opinion of the headmistress of Kidbrooke School: 'All girls, whatever their ability, are able to speak what they know.' Now that it seems likely that we shall have a tunnel or a bridge to span the narrow seas surely we can teach English boys and girls to speak fluently to their Continental neighbours? The essential for success is to teach them in half-classes so that each child can take an active part in oral work. This is a problem of timetabling and must depend on a generous staffing ratio. But if the oral examination were to play an equal part with the written examination at G.C.E. O-level we feel that ways and means could be found of making oral teaching much more effective. Here is a situation in which the reform of the examination might decisively influence the work of teaching in the schools. In Danish schools, under the influence of Otto Jespersen, there have been such oral examinations for many years.

Once the preliminary stages have been surmounted it would be an excellent idea to link the study of a foreign language with the simultaneous study of the geography and history of the country. There should, for example, be a course on French history running concurrently with the study of the French language during one of the terms in the fourth- or fifth-form years. A similar type of geographical course could very well run during the early years when children are being introduced to the language and when they are enthusiastic for the accumulation of 'data' about any topic. One can conceive of a young railway enthusiast accumulating an immense store of knowledge about the Continental railway system and at the same time learning a great deal about the language of one of the Continental countries. Often such a link-up of subjects already takes place. But it would be still more effective if we planned for it to happen.

Our correspondents have suggested that there should be a new and more practical kind of examination for the school-leaver which would provide a real measure of achievement at a less exclusively literary level. Experimentation with such a paper is urgently necessary for the child who has spent four or five years studying French, or any other language, and yet finds himself unable to cope with the essential literariness of the present examinations. In the classroom a great many teachers have been experimenting for many years along these lines, but too often they have been compelled by existing examination requirements to return to the more literary syllabus as the time for G.C.E. has approached. The examination boards should encourage such pioneering work.

An international community lies just ahead of us in which the nation-state will rapidly appear as an interesting historical phenomenon of European history which met its death in the two world wars. The international community born of modern technological communication will require knowledge and tolerance of our neighbours' customs and culture. Language study can play a great part in the gaining of such knowledge.

'Adapt or Perish.' This was the theme of a recent conference held in the House of Commons between members of the All-party Parliamentary Group for World Government and many representatives from all sides of the teaching profession. One speaker went on to say that 'the only people who believed in One World were the Communists and young children'. At the same conference the Chairman of the C.E.W.C.* said that 'what could be done would be by infection rather than by inculcation'. The fact that the annual Christmas conferences of the C.E.W.C. are always heavily oversubscribed proves that children themselves are ready and eager to embrace the idea of One World. It is the traditional curriculum which very often prevents them from pursuing the idea.

In the new-type curriculum current affairs will be taught to all children from the age of fourteen onwards. By bringing current affairs into the timetable where formerly it has been a voluntary extra-curricular activity we shall indicate the importance of a sound basic knowledge of what is going on in other parts of the world, parts which today are no longer intellectually remote from our own country. Since the Press, radio, and above all television are already setting out a great deal of excellent – and some execrable – information on current affairs it is no more than common sense to supply children with this knowledge.

The teaching of current affairs will not be easy. Even the most enlightened Ministries of Education combined with the most philanthropic Educational Trusts will only succeed in exchanging a tiny minority of teachers among the different countries of the world. Children will listen to the man who has

* Council for Education in World Citizenship: a branch of the United Nations catering particularly for school children.

actually visited the country with much more enthusiasm than they will offer to the man who has 'read it up' in the books. But for the great majority who may never have the opportunity to travel the range of accurate information is now immense and growing all the time. Also growing is the availability of native lecturers supplied very often by the cultural departments of embassies as well as by a wide range of voluntary organizations. It would, we believe, be difficult to find a country today which does not devote a good deal of time and energy to 'selling' itself abroad. Why should not schools make use of such programmes?

The cry may go up – What about propaganda, what about indoctrination? The short answer is that it is the job of the teacher running a course on current affairs to know enough about his field to detect the lecturer who is out purely and simply to indoctrinate as opposed to the speaker who merely paints a particular rosy or gloomy picture. But the long-term viewpoint is quite simple. Democracy presupposes the growth and development of children. It is surely far better that attitudes towards other countries, right or wrong, accurate or false, should begin to develop at school and should also begin to change at school under the care of teachers, rather than that children should leave school ignorant of, and bored with other countries and therefore a prey to the first piece of effective propaganda that comes their way.

Equipped with knowledge about the modern world, time must be found for the older children at school to see this world at work. It is now very difficult to arrange a visit to a coal mine for a party of school children. The reason, says the National Coal Board, is simply that every year it arranges for more and more such visits at the requests of schools, and still the demand grows. It is difficult to imagine a more effective way of teaching children about the Industrial Revolution than to take them on such a visit. In the same way they must see the Law Courts at work. Certainly we shall select cases which are suitable for children – certain types of criminal cases do not permit adolescents as spectators – but a visit to the courts will explain much that is obscure when discussed in the classroom. Very few schools can easily visit the House of Commons, but many more older children might be taken to see their local council at work. And a carefully prepared visit to a factory can be of great interest to children who are studying the development of modern industrialism. Where possible we should arrange for children to visit a broadcasting studio, a television studio and a newspaper office, to bring them face to face with the problems of organizing the mass media.

Critics of this book will say that we are utopian. Can any of these things be achieved given the limitations of time and space within which a secondary school has to work? We think that they can if we want to achieve them. We shall point out in Chapter 7 that it is necessary first of all to decrease substantially the pressure of the examination system. We think that democracy will not just survive of its own momentum in this country nor in any other country. But we think that it is possible to educate children in a less cloistered manner than in the past so that by the time they leave school they know enough about their own society to enable them to take an enthusiastic and critical interest in its development. This interest will be stimulated by an awareness of other countries. If the schools can achieve this, it is up to society itself to make sure that such young enthusiasm is given the consideration and respect which it deserves.

About the practice of democracy within the school we have much to say in a later chapter (Chapter 9). But it is obviously important that children should experience approximately the type of school régime which they have been taught to look for in the world around them. For children are shrewd and they can detect insincerity from a long way off – a faculty they owe to their age and inexperience. They will soon know if a school practises what it preaches. A belief in the democratic idea of man and society must therefore be reflected in the régime of the school itself. Fortunately this is now widely believed in every type of English school.

Why is it urgent to prepare children for the responsibilities of democratic citizenship? On 24 August 1958 nine youths, of whom the eldest was twenty and the youngest under sixteen and a half,

> set out on a cruel and vicious manhunt ... armed with iron bars and weapons. ... Their quarry was any man, provided there were not more than two of them together, whose skin happened to be a different colour from their own.(16)

The Notting Hill race riots had begun. All over the Negro world, in Alabama, in Accra, in Lagos, in Leopoldville, and of course in Kingston, Jamaica, Notting Hill was headline news. In a single night's work great damage was done to this country's reputation for equality and protection under the law. The thing that could never happen here, the thing that horrified so much in the Deep South or was so shortly to horrify at Sharpeville, had actually happened. Great Britain, with a population approaching fifty million of whom no more than about 100,000 were Negro immigrants, had suffered race riots. World opinion was profoundly shocked.

But in Britain itself liberal opinion, having approved with some relief the very heavy prison sentences passed on the thugs, ceased to be concerned with the problem. A South African writer commented:

> The truth is that the English liberals are bored, bored, bored – bored with anger, bored with indignation, bored with compassion; and they didn't want to think about the Notting Hill riots precisely because these were the emotions that the events threatened to rouse. Notting Hill showed up once again how thoroughly bored the English liberals are with their own liberalism.(16)

Apart from the work of a few devoted volunteers nothing whatever was done about the conditions in Notting Hill.

But attitudes were formed amongst the young. Some fifteen-year-old girls at a secondary school in West London were asked by their teacher to write frankly their opinions about the riots:*

> I honestly and truthfully hate the coloured people. I admit its our own fault for having them here because when the Queen gave her Christmas Broadcast out over the Radio she said that there was more room at the Inn, but she's alright she won't have them

* The original spelling and punctuation are preserved!

living with her in Buckingham Palace its us kind of people who have to live with them. And its us kind of people who have to bring our children up with the filth there teaching us to live in.[70]

Another girl wrote:

I think coloured people are a load of savages. They are uncivialized, they have got no manner's and no sense of Hygiene. When they come over from their own countries they pinch our Houses and the work that's if they go to work but most of them are just to lazy and live on National Assistance. . . . If I was the ruler of this country and everyone did what I said I would not let one coloured person step foot in England unless they were studing to be a doctor or a nurce and then after learning all they have to make them go back again and stay there.[70]

And another:

I hate them and I would spit on every one if I had the chance. Most of them smell like dog's muck, and eat like dogs to.[70]

These writings speak for themselves. What is more frightening is to consider what kind of people the writers may become and what kind of nonsense they in their turn may instil into their own children.

What contribution can education make to the responsibilities in the home?

'What, if anything, is different about the young today?' – this is the question posed by the able Report of the Labour Party Youth Commission.

The difference, says the Report, lies in the fact that, although all generations have experienced change, never before has a generation grown up under conditions which are so radically different from its predecessor. The Report notes three pieces of evidence to substantiate this claim. First there is the prosperity that awaits the teenager on leaving school. In 1959 the average weekly wage-packet for the male teenager was £5 14s., and for girls under eighteen, £4 7s. 4d. Secondly there is the earlier physical development of children which has led to their reaching sexual maturity at an earlier age.

> A century ago, the average age of puberty in girls was thought to be seventeen. It is now generally experienced at the age of thirteen; in twenty years' time it may be as low as twelve.[76]

Thirdly there has been a considerable change in the cultural climate of young people outside school caused by the growth of the mass media.

> For their interpretation of reality, via the written word, one in two of all young people turn to the *Daily Mirror* during the week and to the *News of the World* on Sunday.[76]

Add to these the fact that the post-war generation is the first to grow up under the shadow of the Bomb, the first to grow up in the age of space travel, the first to witness the political awakening of the African continent, and the first to view a BBC television discussion on the truth or falsehood of the Christian religion – add all these, and much else besides, and there seems little reason to disagree with the Report.

The great merit of the Crowther Report was that it recognized that a great expansion of education would be needed if we were to meet the needs of this new generation (and its successors) and that this expansion would have to be planned many years into the future. If we are, at last, planning a road system for the next twenty years, is it not equally reasonable to plan an educational system for the next twenty years? Without such long-term planning much of our educational effort – speaking in the widest terms – will be wasted. For instance, school must lead on to something else; if for many school-leaving is a dead-end, then it is not surprising that the commercial world will step in, take over the young boy or girl at the age of fifteen or sixteen, and rapidly nullify the effects of education. If there are no decisions about raising the school-leaving age, or establishing County Colleges, or making the Youth Service work, or introducing compulsory day or monthly release, then the younger generation will almost certainly drift, possibly out of control, and certainly farther and farther away from the vital cultural traditions of our civilization. The rise and decline of the Youth Service is a current example of such a policy in drift. In 1939 a pamphlet, *Service to Youth*, went out from the then Board of Education to all local education authorities declaring for the first time that youth welfare was part of the responsibility of a national system of education. In 1944 the Education Act charged the authorities to provide under the Service 'facilities for recreation and social and physical training' and at the same time the McNair Committee suggested that there should be a full-time Youth Service personnel of between 5,000 and 6,000 trained leaders. But in 1959 there were perhaps not more than 700 youth leaders and the government was unable to spend more than three to four million pounds on the Youth Service – about half one per cent of the Ministry of Education's annual budget. And yet the Youth Service is still the only provision made for the school-leaver.

To put the point bluntly: as far as the school-leaver is concerned the government has just not given a damn.(76)

The point is this. The responsibilities of adult society cannot be learnt during four or even six short, crowded years in a secondary school. Certain foundations can be laid, certain attitudes and values can, with most children, be built up. But without a national policy for education at least as all-embracing, in its own fashion, as the policies of the private sector of education, much of the school effort will be wasted. Mr Butler once said that he thought it would take twenty years to implement his Act; seventeen years have now gone by!

Can schools make a significant contribution to preparing boys and girls for the responsibilities of starting homes and families of their own? Educate a woman and you educate a family – so the old saying goes. Recent correspondence in *The Times* (January to February 1960) on the subject of education for girls revealed clearly that more thought should be given to the curriculum for girls. The curriculum of 'soft options' for girls is no longer preached by any but a handful of reactionaries and only from the secure isolation of the club armchair. But the alternative which is to provide girls with a curriculum that differs in no way from the boys' curriculum is equally unsatisfactory. Many girls today expect to become career women as well as wives and mothers, and they need a curriculum designed to prepare them for this dual role in society.

> In a way women, who are less obsessed than men are with careers today, are the last upholders of liberal education, pursued not for gain but for its own sake.(55)

The increasingly push-button home of the future will provide more leisure time for married women. At the same time the earlier marriage age and longer living will give women far greater opportunities to enjoy their leisure. Many more women will have the experience of starting a career, teaching for example, and returning to it when their children no longer need their daily care. And there will be women who pursue full careers as equal partners (or competitors) with men. The girls' curriculum must be broad enough to cater for all these needs.

Whereas the boys' curriculum must lead towards a specialized field within a broad general education, the girls' curriculum should lead towards a broad general education with a specialized field attached to it. For example, it is the girls who teach in the primary schools. Most important for this work is the personality and versatility of the teacher, including the gift of understanding children. A girl who is to achieve these qualities requires a good general education with ample opportunities for developing her mind and her emotions. But at the same time we should remember that all primary-school teachers introduce children to mathematics. Therefore girls who wish to take up teaching as a career should receive a really good mathematical training themselves. For a primary-school teacher the art of teaching elementary mathematics therefore becomes a speciality. Probably the shortage of mathematics lecturers in training colleges, which is specially acute in women's colleges, is one of the greatest bottlenecks in our whole framework of education.

What should be the ingredients of a broad general education

for girls? Surely the criterion should be that it is sufficiently unspecialized and informal to encourage the greatest development of girls' personalities. This we have not yet achieved except in a handful of schools. Female education still seeks to impose upon our girls a series of lessons that are too remote and de-personalized. More especially is this true of the single-sex secondary schools, where the curriculum tends to ape the boys' schools and where imaginative experimentation is too often discouraged. It appears to be less true of the newer secondary schools where co-education has become the practice rather than the exception and in which much valuable experimentation in curricula is taking place.

It is rather a pathetic thought that until modern times pronouncements about girls' education should so often have assumed that training for the care of homes and families should encompass no more than the teaching of the domestic subjects. These subjects should probably comprise about a third of the girls' curriculum and should include such things as simple practical science, dietetics, First Aid, and household accounting. If the future should see the return of more married women into teaching after a period of home-making and caring for young children, as indeed it must if we are to staff girls' schools adequately, there is every chance that the more practical side of a girl's education will benefit from their experience.

Women can be expert in the domestic crafts, but their homes can yet lack much that goes towards the upbringing of families. For they are asked to do more than the 101 practical things that fall to their lot day by day. The English subjects and the fine arts should be basic to the girls' curriculum. So much, indeed almost all, of a child's early culture is learnt from his mother. Modern psychology has attached a unique importance to these early years in a child's life. How many children gain the richest experience of their early childhood from the immense advantage that accrues to them from the well-stocked mind of their mother? It is more important in girls' education than in boys' that the great cultural subjects should be treated to sufficient depth to enable them to retain a lifelong enthusiasm for the 'arts' of life and in sufficient breadth to help them to communicate this enthusiasm to their own children.

Science and in particular theoretical science appeals less to girls than to boys, although we do not exclude the possibility that more girls will in the future be attracted to science. This will depend on the way in which science is publicized as a career for girls. It will also depend on getting a much larger proportion of really able scientists to teach in girls' schools. In the early years science taught to girls should tend to be practical rather than theoretical.

For the careers which girls take up immediately after leaving school the aim should be to provide a broad general education which includes the gaining of some specialized knowledge in the field of their choice, for example through pre-nursing or secretarial courses. More often than boys, who still have a greater incentive than girls to go on to higher education, girls stay on for only a single year in the sixth form. It is quite vital that girls who stay on for this single year should not find themselves embarked, whether they like it or not, upon the preliminary stages of the full G.C.E. A-level course. They need a first-class year of general education with enough time to treat topics of their choice in greater depth than has been possible before. Such a general course we have outlined in our proposals for the Complementary Level of the G.C.E. (see page 141 ff. and Diagram 4). The Complementary Level would contain approximately half of the factual content of the A-level syllabuses when these A-level syllabuses have themselves been pruned of their present luxuriance. At Complementary Level a sixth-form girl, whether she proceeded to the examination or not, would be able to take two or three non-specialized subjects during her first year in the sixth and add another two or three if she then decided to stay on for a second year. It is interesting to note that in the comprehensive schools, where large staffs have made it possible to provide such first-class general education in the sixth form, there is less reluctance amongst girls to stay on into the sixth.

In the sixth form, for girls who desire to specialize and go to the university or to enter one of the professions, the curriculum will follow closely that of the boys with similar ambitions, and these are discussed together in Chapter 6.

A further point about education for girls. The earlier physical maturity to which we drew attention at the beginning of this section cannot be ignored when we consider the social community of the girls' school. Why should we not make education fashionable in the same way as good grooming for girls has now become fashionable throughout the length and breadth of the land? The atmosphere of the sixth form in the girls' school should now come closer to the atmosphere of the young adult world. Girls will not stay on unless they feel that sixth-form education is an asset to them in their efforts to make their way in this world. The headmistresses who find the time to fit the occasional dress show into their sixth-form curriculum, the schools which provide facilities and time for girls to learn the skills of entertaining their friends, the teachers who take the trouble to discuss with older girls the problems and opportunities of the adult world – these are all on the right lines. During the later stages of their schooling girls are already young women and rightly expect to be treated accordingly.

Parents are partners with the schools in the education of their children. The right curriculum in our secondary schools we have found in essence to be a broader and more varied curriculum than that which obtains at the moment. Mr M. L. Jacks has gone so far as to say that a 'revolution' is required in the curriculum before girls will get the education they deserve. The new type of curriculum will certainly require great changes in secondary schools. Parents who were themselves educated under the old type of curriculum and who undoubtedly received an education that was inadequate in both quality and quantity cannot be expected to understand or sympathize with the new type of education unless a real effort is made on the part of the schools to keep them in the picture.

American exchange teachers to this country have frequently commented upon the lack of communication between parents and schools. Recently this was confirmed in a sample inquiry carried out with 734 families in the Greater London area and, on a smaller scale, in Northampton.

> It is a striking fact that a third of the mothers with children at school feel they would like to be told more about what goes on at school or to be given more opportunity to discuss their children with the school.(41)

In a real sense American parents regard themselves as the owner-managers of their public schools. From colonial days the 'schoolhouse' has been a proud possession of the community and a first call upon the public purse. In England, where public education developed much later than in America, parents have traditionally looked upon the school as something imposed upon their liberty to do what they like with their children. Since the war this traditional attitude has changed. Parents now want their children to receive the best possible education. But many schools still keep their parents at arms' length and tell them very little about what is going on in the school.

How do we promote more contact between parents and schools? Parent-Teacher Associations are opposed by some heads because they develop along the wrong lines. We feel that this is an inadequate reason for not developing them at all. Perhaps they will be more successful if their role is clearly delimited in advance, possibly by legislation. For example, no member of a Parent-Teacher Association should be entitled to make use of his privileged position to attack the policy of the school in the Press or on radio or television. By its very nature a school is not subject to the normal process of public criticism. It is not an adult society and cannot be subjected to adult rules and regulations. Parents have a sufficient channel for complaint and criticism by recourse to the local authority which runs the school. But provided its role is clarified we think that a Parent-Teacher Association has much to contribute to a school. A good association should make many parents feel that they belong to the school where their child is being educated. This feeling will very rapidly communicate itself to the child and a division of loyalties, which can do so much to delay progress in adolescence, will be avoided.

For its part it is the duty of the school, probably the specific duty of the careers teacher, to keep the parents fully informed about the careers which are available to their children. Such information is commonly quite inadequate today. Much talent is still wasted because of early school-leaving or refusal to take the opportunities now becoming available in further education. For instance we have a seventy-million-pound building plan for 'technical and continued education'. Interviewed about this plan, Dr George Brossan, Director of Technical Education for Middlesex, said:

> Many parents, thinking back to their own youth, speak disparagingly of *further education*. The trouble is that they won't see that times have changed.(18)

There is a possibility that the parents of the next generation – today's school-leavers – may think differently. But until that happy position is reached schools and education authorities must do their best to enlighten today's parents.

What sort of help can parents expect from schools in the upbringing of their children? Quite frequently a school prospectus, which is all the information that most parents have about the school, sets out a good deal of useful information. It discusses the academic courses which the child may follow, the arrangements which the school can make for the child when the time comes to choose a career, and the activities outside the classroom such as clubs and sports. But the prospectus seldom includes anything about the social organization of the school and the standards of behaviour which the school expects of the children. To include a short discussion of these matters in the prospectus would require careful wording, but we think it would be of great help to parents.

The great majority of parents like to feel that the school is committed to a policy towards behaviour that is at least as high as the standards they have taught the child at home. An obvious example amongst boys is the question of smoking. Parents who do not wish their sons to smoke at home until they have reached years of discretion are entitled to feel that the school will enforce the same rule at all times, particularly of course when the boys are off the school premises on visits and expeditions. And it is reasonable that parents who don't mind their sons smoking at home should know that they will not be allowed to smoke while they are under school discipline. More important than this, however, is the teaching of good manners. In the mass, and in a hurry, as children quickly discover, our behaviour towards each other rapidly deteriorates. Tempers become frayed and unhappiness and even serious emotional troubles can develop. Parents who have built up their homes on the basis of mutual respect and kindliness between their children wish such standards to be consciously fostered at school. Unlike some of the Victorians we now believe that children are essentially good-natured and it is not difficult to persuade most of them to behave in this way. But a school has to plan its social organization carefully in order to allow them to do so.

The development of the child's personality, which is the core of education, cannot be completed within the walls of the school building. For many children approaching the end of their school career there is a sharp contrast between the organized life of the school and the freedom of the holidays. A school must impose a good deal of discipline upon children and the relaxation of this discipline often comes too suddenly for the equilibrium of the child. This is probably one reason for the steep rise in juvenile delinquency during the last year of compulsory schooling. For ten years a child's life is organized and towards the end a reaction inevitably sets in. The only way to counteract this tendency is to provide, during the holidays and after school-leaving, a wide variety of activities for young people.

The kind of activity that is required for the older child has been admirably defined in the Duke of Edinburgh's Award:

> The urge to be somebody and do something is inherent in human nature. If this motive force is to be effective, it must be crystallized

into a clear aim. The future of our civilization will depend on the ability and willingness of the young people of today to make it their purpose to prepare themselves to give their best service to the community; yet modern inventions and ways of life tend to encourage them to put their own interests first. The need to help the young generation, first to discover their talents and then to use them in the service of others, is a matter which should concern us all.[14]

The awards are based very carefully upon two principles: the discovery of children's talents and their use in service to other people. To gain an award a boy or girl* must successfully complete a programme in four kinds of activity: rescue or public-service training, an expedition, the learning of an art or craft, and physical fitness. The scheme is administered by voluntary organizations and much of the preparation and testing is conducted by bodies and institutions which can offer their own experience and the facilities for testing children. Here is one of the imaginative experiments in the whole field of modern education.

Parents, we feel, have a great part to play in fostering this kind of holiday activity. In fact without their active support we doubt whether it will be possible to increase substantially the number of children who are involved in such activities. Many teachers give a great deal of voluntary service both in and out of school terms to these activities. But all teachers, if they are to remain really effective, need holidays – whether working or not – when they can get right away from the problems of adolescent children. Nor can it all be left to those who are employed full-time in the Youth Service or in any other form of service to youth. During the last war many an Englishman surprised himself at the sort of voluntary work which he found himself carrying out and which he had not remotely conceived of himself as doing in the years of disillusion. Can we not persuade many more people to come in and help in this particular way to bring up the younger generation?

In secondary schools we envisage a Parents' Association

* The award scheme was preceded by a pilot scheme which was confined to boys.

which would provide the fulcrum for holiday activities. It would be their duty, and for many their pleasure, to cater for the needs of the children. Working, we suggest, with a particular member of the school staff (holiday service master?), the association would get to know children who wanted, for instance, to go in for the award scheme. The association would hold regular open meetings at the end of the school day when the opportunities and details of holiday schemes could be discussed. The association would be responsible for administering holiday schemes and on occasion some of its members would, we think, enjoy initiating and leading holiday activities of their own devising. The association would need a small fund for such things as correspondence and travel expenses. It should also be a legally constituted body, as often as not a committee of the Parent-Teacher Association. Once such an association were established in schools we believe that there would be many more children wanting to participate in activities.

Rejecting, as we must, a compulsory state youth service we can solve the problem of building up character and adaptability in children by a massive extension of voluntary effort. Recently it has become fashionable to write letters to the papers deploring the character of the younger generation. To all these letter writers and many more we now offer an opportunity to do something about it.

> If only a small part of the ingenuity, inventiveness, and creativeness now devoted to the sale of commercial goods to the 'teenage market' were directed towards encouraging the activities of well-run youth organizations, then much might be done to remedy the present state of futility, boredom, and lethargic apathy in which so many young people today spend their leisure time.(67)

> Education can only function within the broad directives of right and wrong which society gives.(44)

Clearly schools are deeply concerned with training children for their responsibilities in their homes both now as children and later on as parents. To us it is just as clear that schools alone are not equal to the task. In the private sector of education this has been realized for a long time. Modern conditions which have brought more money, earlier physical maturity, and the mass media to children, make it imperative that our society should accept more responsibility for the ethical and moral training of the young. Quite rightly children will not listen to our advice if we merely offer it paternalistically and then continue at the same time to ignore their vital needs. These needs do not stop when children leave the classrooms at the end of the day; nor do they suddenly cease when the holidays begin; nor do they disappear when children leave school. Today's children have immense reserves of talent and great potentiality for service. On them we must pin our hopes of the more civilized community of the future. But in order to do this we must draw upon our own reserves and we must display to them our own capacity for service.

Are conditions really any different today? We consider that it is the pace of change which is different.

> In recent years new and powerful influences have begun to reshape our society. Values are changing and the impact of the change is felt most of all by the young.[76]

Broadly speaking we have to learn to use our new-found material advantages for our own spiritual enrichment and for the benefit of the less fortunate people in the world. A couldn't-care-less materialistic approach to life would lead us into ways far distant from the main currents of our civilization. Almost certainly such an approach would ensure our decadence and eclipse as a great people.

In this chapter we are suggesting that the attitude of society to young people must also change. If it does not we shall fail to pass on to the younger generation its heritage.

How well equipped is a child when he leaves school to become a self-supporting member of the community?

Nothing is more perplexing to the school-leaver than the future. Since he entered the primary school ten years or more before, the child has spent his working life in the same kind of environment. During all these years his life has been organized for him by grown-ups. His standard of behaviour, his work, and his play, have all been prescribed for him. In most cases his emotional development has taken place in an atmosphere of security. His time has been planned for him and certain standards of achievement have been placed clearly in front of him. Of necessity, because he is a child, he has been held only partly responsible for his own decisions. In childhood we live mostly for the present, rarely in the past, and hesitatingly in the future. Often school-leavers appear sure of themselves and sophisticated in a jejune way. What we do not always remember is that this sophistication may hide a deep anxiety about themselves and the future.

Education has the very important task of preparing them to meet this future; to meet not only the weeks and months that immediately follow school-leaving but also the years that lie ahead. Education of itself cannot complete this task. A man cannot blame his education if he never succeeds in balancing his budget, nor can he blame his school if he spends his life in a factory when all the time he would really like to be a farmer. In our civilization men and women are free to do what they like with their lives and, if we must blame, we are only at liberty to blame ourselves. But a man can expect that his education will prepare him for the choices that he will have to make and equip him with the basic information without which he cannot choose effectively. If he must look back, education should ensure that he does not look back in anger.

The choice of a satisfying career depends upon making an accurate assessment of the child's aptitude and abilities. This is an important part of a teacher's job. At school a child is under continuous observation by his teachers. A broad curriculum, which is what this book proposes, should enable children to be observed while they are studying a wide range of intellectual disciplines. Our discussion of the school community (see Chapter 9) emphasizes the equally important point that they must participate in a range of extra-curricular activities when they will also be under observation. Provided the organization of the school ensures that each child will be the particular responsibility of a particular teacher during the various stages of his school life, it should be possible to make a comprehensive assessment of his aptitudes and abilities. Such an assessment the child will take with him when he leaves on his leaving certificate. This is the assessment which will guide his parents when the time comes to choose a career. When parents discuss their child with teachers they are often surprised to find that the teachers have discovered qualities in the child which they did not know existed. Such discoveries are an important contribution which the school must make to the future of the child.

'An interesting career with good opportunities for advancement is offered....' – so run the advertisements in the newspapers. Behind a few lines of print lies a decision that may determine the work of many years, perhaps of a lifetime. This is a modern phenomenom of industrial society. Thousands of years of drudgery in which men and women worked at jobs which were not of their own choosing have been replaced by a society which can offer a vast range of jobs from which to choose. Many of these jobs require technical training of a high order which must be acquired by the child when he begins to work at the job itself. We are discussing the schools which undertake the education of the most intelligent forty per cent of the nation's children, and it is not the task of these schools to give children vocational training for their jobs. But we can and should guide them in their choice of career.

Schools should have one or more senior teachers charged with the specific duty of helping children to choose a career which will give full scope to their aptitudes and abilities. Clothing the bare bones of the brochures and pamphlets, put out by industry and the professions for their would-be entrants, is not easily done, especially when one remembers that very few teachers have had any experience of the careers that they are talking about. Children want to know a great deal more than the entrance qualifications for a particular job. They want to know the sort of way in which they will be using their mind.

They want to know how the early stages of the job will give place as time goes on to the wider field of interest and responsibility. They want to know the salary structure of each career and how it compares with other similar careers. They want to consider what kind of working life they will have in any particular job. These are some of the considerations which they should have before them.

During the later school years the curriculum must allow time for the discussion of careers. Often the teachers concerned with careers will invite speakers to come and talk during periods on current affairs. Today the planning of these talks is very often haphazard, depending on the availability of the speaker or the necessity to fill in a period in the timetable towards the end of the term. There should be a planned series of talks on careers to be given to all children during their last year at school. Arranging such a series of talks will very often be beyond the individual resources of all but the experienced careers member of staff. We consider that the Parents' Association (see page 123) could help a great deal. The association will contain representatives from a wide range of careers in industry, commerce, and the professions. These are the people on whom the careers teacher can draw for his speakers. In a single school year there is no reason why children should not hear a dozen talks on the possible careers which are open to them – each talk from an authority who is himself working in the field.

Seeing the world at work in factory, farm, or shipyard is also an essential element in making up one's mind about a career. Liaison between personnel managers and schools can be most effective. We should like to see a day every term for school visits to factories. Many independent schools use at least one day per term for training in the Combined Cadet Forces. Factory visits are also important. A period of holiday work for older schoolchildren can be even more interesting and rewarding. Of course there are difficulties in providing such work. Many industrial jobs are well beyond the capabilities of untrained children. Harm rather than good may be done if children spend a fortnight in a factory or office making cups of tea and getting in the way. They may be permanently frightened away from potentially interesting jobs. Holiday work for older school-children will need careful planning and liaison among all those concerned. But if industry will accept the responsibility for such planning and work out the types of programme that children could follow, they would gain good opportunities for experiencing the conditions under which their careers might be lived. In the long run it would be to the advantage of industrial management to build up closer relations with schools.

For the majority who leave school at the age of fifteen or sixteen it will be necessary to staff the Youth Employment Service much more adequately. At the moment there are not more than 900 youth employment officers to cope with about 500,000 school-leavers every year; the number of school-leavers will also increase during the next few years. One employment officer for more than 500 children who are starting on their first job. Is this really enough? How much time will the employment officer have for becoming really well informed about changing conditions in local industries? How much time will he have for the occasional follow-up of a doubtful starter in some particular job? A boy or girl may try two or three jobs before settling down to a steady one: these will provide him with variety of experience. But it is not uncommon for a boy to run through fifteen or twenty jobs in the years immediately after leaving school. This can scarcely be a good thing for him or provide him with the kind of experience that will enable him to work well in later years. The choice of career must be

> Right for their own future happiness and the development of their talents, and right because it enables them to make the best contribution to their community.[13]

This will not happen unless heads of schools accept their responsibility for the guidance of children when they choose their careers. In view of the complexity of the choice heads should delegate such responsibility to one or more of their senior members of staff. These teachers will need an allotment of time for the job, secretarial assistance, and a little money for travelling expenses. A job such as this will depend to a great extent upon the personal contacts that the teacher can build up with the local industries and professions and with the Parents' Association. It will be a job best done by a teacher intending to spend some considerable time at the same school. For many teachers this job might prove to be the most rewarding of their career. It is a job not dissimilar to the housemaster's job in a public school. For what can be more rewarding than the knowledge that one has played a significant part in enabling a child to make a happy and useful start to his career?

We consider that new thought, followed by action, is urgently needed over girls' careers. In the first place girls do not get their fair share of the meagre allotment of university places.

> In 1957 31 per cent of all A-level passes in the G.C.E. examination were gained by girls ... in 1957–8 [in the universities] there were 17,404 out of 73,563 girls or 23·5 per cent.(65)

Observers of the university scene have been quick to point out that the magisterial progress of Churchill College for the promotion of science and technology has contrasted with the difficult career of New Hall, the first new college for women to be opened in Cambridge for many years. The era of increasing specialization in sixth forms has borne more heavily upon girls' schools than upon the boys'. This specialization has faced many girls' schools with the cruel dilemma of either sacrificing the artistic and general studies which should form an essential part of girls' education or continuing with these studies and sacrificing the hope of gaining university places. It is easier for a boy to make up in later life for the general education which did not come his way at school than it is for a girl.

In the second place not nearly enough thought has been given to the pattern of a girl's life and its relationship to a career. Equal pay for women is the slogan under which the emancipators have been fighting during the thirty years that have followed the achievement of women's suffrage. The slogan today should be equal opportunity for women. Opportunity for women must not only mean opportunity for unmarried women to pursue a career in no way inferior to men, but it must also mean opportunity for married women to take up a career after marriage. Time and again married women of considerable intelligence and ability find that they wish to take up a career by the time their children are at secondary school. Sometimes it is the career which they were engaged upon before marriage; sometimes it is a new career for which they feel that the experience of marriage and bringing up a family has particularly suited them. In either case they soon discover that it is not easy to do so. In particular there are few facilities for training, retraining, or just taking a refresher course to bring them up to date in their profession. We touch here upon the problems of adult education. Women's careers depend upon part-time facilities being available for them to take training or refresher courses while running their own homes.

The economics of everyday life should find a place in the curriculum of the school-leaver. Contrary to some opinion teachers are often well informed about this topic – an advantage that accrues to all members of underpaid professions. A child leaves school and becomes a wage-earner. Not many years may elapse before he also becomes a married man and the father of a family. He and his wife will need to know how to draw up their family budget, how to buy a house, and whether they can afford a motor-car. They want to be able to estimate the cost of having children. The happiness of their married life will depend greatly upon their ability to make a sound estimate of their economic position and to act accordingly. Inevitably they will discover a great deal at a later stage by trial and error, but they can be better prepared at school than they have been in the past.

For the sixth-former the non-specialized courses at C-level (see Diagram 4, page 143) should provide a deeper insight into everyday life. These courses, which will invariably be one-year rather than two-year courses, will be available to children who are studying for both A-level and C-level. The only difference will be that the A-level child will have less time for such courses. These non-specialist subjects, of which thirteen in all are listed in Diagram 4, can easily be used to take even the one-year sixth-former a considerable way behind the façade of modern life. A child who spends four or five periods a week doing *political* studies, begins at the same time to find out about *commercial* or *statistical mathematics*, and also takes a course on *art* or *music*, will probably spend about half his time each week being taught, and a third of his time studying privately in the sixth-form library. If the child then likes sixth-form work and decides to stay on for a second year, he can switch to another three-subject combination, say *use of English language and literature*, *social studies* or *modern language and European culture*, and *impact of science on modern life and thought*; again his time will be divided between work in the classroom and in the library. At the end of two such years he will be a great deal more widely informed about the modern world than the present sixth-former.

Once the idea of the non-specialist course for sixth-formers becomes accepted schools will obviously devise a wider variety of courses to suit their particular environment and to make full use of the talents of their staff. Why should so many people remain ignorant about the law and its relationship to everyday life? A few years ago a fascinating book was published called *John Citizen and the Law*.[49] On the day of publication – how fortunate that it was a cheap book! – a technical college purchased 1,200 copies for use as a text-book. This book would provide excellent material for a non-specialized sixth-form course. *John Citzen and the Law* was written by Ronald Rubinstein, after a lifetime's experience as a solicitor. Similar books, written perhaps by practising professional men and women rather than by professional writers, could be produced on the same theme of the relation of professional experience to everyday life. They might very well provide the right kind of material for the sixth form.

This chapter has dealt with the new-type curriculum during the later years at school and with special emphasis upon the demands that society will make upon the young adult soon after he leaves school. We have pointed towards the topics with which this curriculum should be concerned, we have suggested the kind of approach which should be made towards the child and his work during these years, and we have made specific suggestions for new courses of study. We have also indicated that the demands of society cannot be met without a change in the attitude of society itself towards young people. Much of what we have described is being attempted by individual schools. Now is the time to give it wider application.

CHAPTER 6

The Sixth Form

WHAT is the great debate on the sixth form about? Is it just another example of how teachers prefer to discuss topics that lie within their Lilliputian world rather than enter the realms of men? During the last decade more ink and paper has been expended on this theme than on any other aspect of education, always excepting the 11-plus examination. What is it all about?

Foreigners will tell with envy that their education is the poorer for not having an English type of sixth form. What have they got in mind? The two essential features of the English sixth form are atmosphere and speciality. The atmosphere which exists in a good sixth form is an intellectual atmosphere. Ten years of learning mental drills and techniques now gives place – and this is important – for the first time to learning how to use the mind. That is why sixth-form work is immediately distinguishable to the child by its greater freedom and greater responsibility. That is why sixth-form work is no longer bounded by the arbitrary frontiers of text-books. That is why the part played by the memory is lessened in the sixth form. That is why children are encouraged to argue with each other and with their teachers. They are learning to think for themselves.

At this point, in the English system, children begin to specialize. The arguments for such specialization rest on two premises, one old and one new. The old, which underlay the nineteenth-century classical education, was the premise that the awakening mind can be most effectively trained by the study of a limited field of knowledge which contains within itself the utmost capacity for general application. In the Classical tradition this training depended upon the sixth-form teacher having, himself, these qualifications. In the opinion of one he 'needs to be widely read – apart from his own specialities – in theology, English, history, current affairs, and most aspects of European culture and civilization'.[28] Such demands require men and women of high intellectual calibre and it is these people, both in the past and today, who set the standards of the sixth form.

The new premise is of an entirely different order and it entered the sixth form when scientific education began to establish itself. It is simply this: that knowledge, and mainly scientific knowledge, is increasing all the time and therefore children must specialize more if they are to keep in the race. Special knowledge, says this line of argument, is increasing all the time; therefore children must begin earlier, specialize harder, and go on longer. Ultimately it comes down to a matter of sheer quantity, as in the American TV programmes where a candidate offers himself for questioning by a panel on any aspect of one subject and on nothing else at all. An old woman recently won a substantial prize for her knowledge of the works and life of Charles Dickens, but she had never heard of D. H. Lawrence! This is the new premise of specialization.

Today both the atmosphere and the speciality of the old ideal of the sixth form are under great strain. The most important reason for this strain is the number of children who now stay on into the sixth. Thirty or forty years ago a sixth-form teacher might have had fifteen or twenty children and, with the more generous staffing of those days, plenty of time to teach them. His work was conducted on something very like the tutorial system at Oxford or Cambridge – for which universities it was largely a preparation. Usually, because they were mostly potential scholars, his sixth form could be taught as a homogeneous group of companion intellects. Now there are many more children who have all rightly been encouraged to continue their education in the sixth form. Amongst these sixth-formers there will be ability ranging from the potential scholar, through the slightly above average, to the child who wants to stay for one year in the sixth in order to broaden his mind before taking a job. How is the sixth-form teacher to help them all while preserving at the same time the essential intellectual atmosphere of his work?

The strain has been augmented by the advance of the new premise for specialization. Quantity has replaced quality in the syllabuses for the Advanced Level of the G.C.E. For instance, it is now generally felt that nothing less than a twenty-five per cent reduction in all science syllabuses will suffice if sixth forms are to receive a more general education. How far has specialization in science actually gone? It does not look as bad as some critics have feared if we consider the timetable only, but if we include homework the amount of specialization is seen to be enormous. If we further include extra-curricular activities we often find that they are closely connected with the specialist subjects: for example biologists with natural history societies, physicists with radio societies, or more broadly scientists with scientific societies. Desirable as these activities are they tend to accentuate the bias towards specialization. In Diagram 3 we illustrate the present degree of specialization in science sixths; at the same time we indicate the broadening that could be achieved for both science and arts specialists by a twenty-five-per-cent reduction of syllabuses. Doubly unfortunate has been the fact that, during the time when all sixth-form disciplines have been under quantitative pressure, there has also been an acute shortage of university places in this country (see Table 1, page 29). University places depend upon the results of the A-level examinations, not, except fortuitously, upon the general education of the child. Therefore the old, somewhat leisured, sixth form of the past has been replaced by a sixth which has become more intensely specialist-minded in the sense that this means the accumulation of specialist knowledge for the purposes of the A-level examination. A future historian, thinks Mr T. E. B. Howarth, will classify this epoch

> as the period of the professional revolution, the age when nothing was left to chance, when the sheer weight of the curriculum flattened out curiosity, when the hungry sheep looked up and were gorged.(29)

Diagram 3 *Degree of Specialization in the Sixth Form*

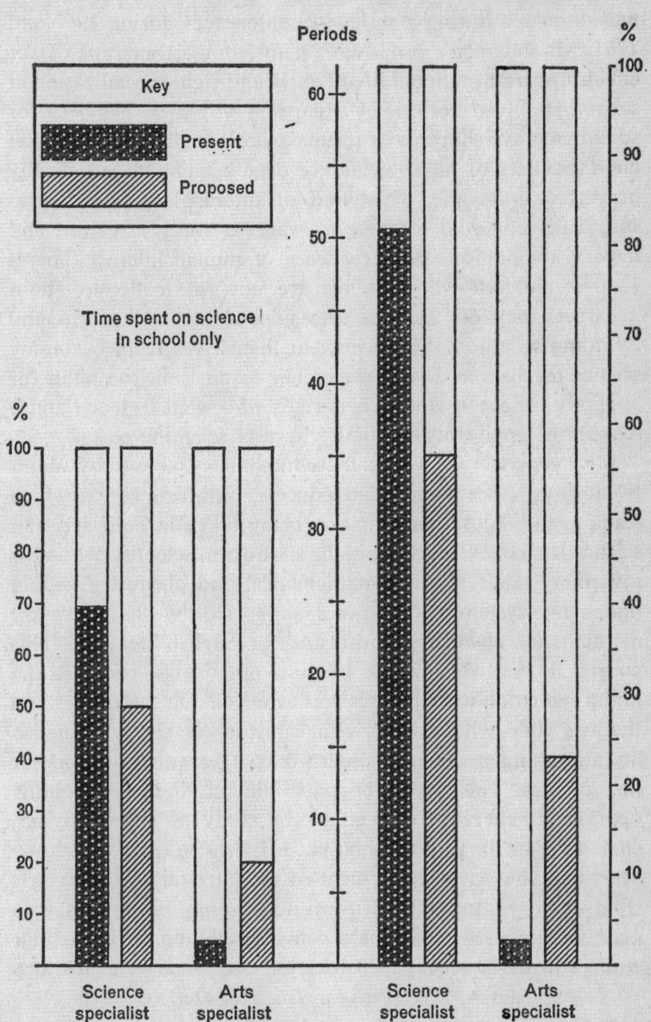

The first constructive proposals for adapting sixth-form education to modern needs have been those put forward by Mr A. D. C. Peterson in a Report to the Gulbenkian Foundation (38) and discussed during a series of conferences during 1960 and 1961. Mr Peterson's proposals* stem from his analysis of the effects upon our national life of early and rigid specialization at school. He illustrates this by discussing why there has been for so long a grave shortage of science teachers. He points out that good teachers of all subjects are deeply and sympathetically interested in people. This kind of interest, says Mr Peterson, leads potential teachers to want to study literature and history, the subjects *par excellence* of human interest. Therefore as children whose minds are not yet made up about a career, they opt for the arts side of the sixth form and by doing so automatically prevent themselves from becoming science teachers at a later stage. The result is all too plain for anybody to see: a glut of historians who want to teach and a scarcity of applicants of quality for any scientific post.

Mr Peterson's answer is to reduce all syllabuses by about twenty-five per cent and to introduce a sixth-form course which leads to the A-level examination being taken in both arts and science subjects. For example the sixth-form scientist, who now invariably takes physics, mathematics, and chemistry, would under his system take physics supported by the necessary mathematics, chemistry, and history or English literature. This course, he considers, would be quite practicable, provided the initial reduction in syllabuses was achieved. On the other hand the arts child who may now take history or classics, English literature, and perhaps a modern language, would add one of the sciences. This would be more difficult because scientific opinion is generally opposed to the study of either physics, chemistry, or biology in isolation. Mr Peterson suggests, however, that the scientific element in the curriculum of the arts child could be made up with either biology or physics with mathematics. Obviously there can be variations of particular courses in particular sixth forms, but the principle of his idea

* See also A. D. C. Peterson, *Educating Our Rulers.*(40)

will remain – that children will take A-level, specializing in subjects from both the arts and the sciences.

The second proposal for the adaptation of the sixth form has been the suggestion that 'general studies' should become an integral part of sixth-form work and that university selectors should in future regard it as such. Opinion divides on the advisability of making general studies an examinable subject at A-level. The Northern Universities Joint Matriculation Board have already introduced general studies as one of a three-subject option at A-level, but it is too early yet to assess its results. Another group is working on the construction of a general studies course which would include four intellectual fields – 'historical and social, aesthetic, scientific and technological, and moral, religious, and philosophical'.(17) Such a course would be worked on an experimental basis for a year or two by a number of schools and it is hoped that it would lead to the drawing up of agreed syllabuses and examinations. The adoption of general studies in the sixth form would mean that children would continue their present specialization in the arts or the sciences, and that their general education would be undertaken in general studies periods, which might then be taken as a full subject at A-level. Thus specialization would be offset by a broader study.

On 30 June 1961 *The Times Educational Supplement* reported a further move towards a broader sixth-form curriculum. The headmasters of twenty-one of the leading public, grammar, and comprehensive schools dispatched 1,300 copies of a draft of *An Agreement to Broaden the Curriculum* to heads of secondary schools. The draft makes two proposals for sixth forms: first that all children should have a range of choices open to them on both arts and science sides when they enter the sixth form; second that after entry into the sixth form all children should devote at least one-third of their periods to subjects other than those in which they are specializing. The draft proposed that schools which signed the Agreement should be known by name to the universities and other institutions of higher education so that candidates for admission to these institutions should be known to come from the 'ABC' schools. The avowed object of the draft was to enlist sufficient support to enable the schools to carry through a broader sixth-form education without in any way prejudicing the chances of their candidates for admission to higher education.

These proposals have grave drawbacks as a possible basis for sixth-form education over the next decade. Mr Peterson's proposal takes no account of the wide range of ability in a sixth form today. By suggesting that children should specialize in both the arts and the sciences he has achieved a break-through between the present isolation of children in their sixth-form speciality. If 'two cultures' do in fact exist, and if the gap is growing wider between them, then Mr Peterson's suggestions may help to diminish it. But he has achieved this at the expense of more over-loading of the curriculum. By no means do the majority of the present teachers of the humanities concede that their syllabuses are too large at A-level. Consequently they will fight hard to prevent too much pruning of syllabuses, with the result that, even if there is a substantial pruning of scientific syllabuses, the A-level subjects proposed by Mr Peterson would be a formidable proposition. Many teachers regard Mr Peterson's proposal as unrealistic for all but an intelligent minority of sixth-formers.

In rejecting the second solution – that of examinable general studies as an A-level subject – we take our stand on the fact that 'Subject-mindedness . . . is one of the marks of the sixth form'.(44) We think there is great value in the English tradition of study in depth of a limited range of subjects and we do not think that this can be achieved by general studies papers which must inevitably parcel out great fields of knowledge in neatly tied paper packages for pre-digested consumption.

Let us restate the problem. Sixth-form education as it was conceived by English teachers of the past and as we have inherited it today is under strain from two sources. The first is that we must now cater for much larger sixth forms – six times as many children as in 1938 now take mathematics at A-level

– and for sixth forms of a much wider range of ability. The second is that as knowledge increases, particularly in the scientific and technological field, there is very strong pressure bearing upon schools to begin specialization earlier and in the sixth form to specialize much harder and more rigidly. The casualties from these pressures are likely to be the less able of the sixth-formers. Very often today these are first-generation grammar-school children staying on into the sixth form. For them and their parents the whole business is very much of a venture and they will neither stay long nor get hold of the idea of sixth-form education in its broad sense if they meet merely with rigid specialization and grinding preparation for examinations. But we need them desperately and we cannot afford to let them drift away. The other casualty has already been 'general education'. The classical ideal of the well-read and well-informed sixth form has gone. 'By the time I had left Eton,' writes Cyril Connolly, 'I knew by heart something of the literature of five civilizations.' [10] Not a bad achievement considering literature was not taught at Eton at that time! We cannot expect the same today, for we must construct a new concept of 'general education' which includes both arts and sciences rather than arts alone.

Our proposals, based on an idea first put forward by the headmaster of Winchester, are specifically designed to meet the current pressures upon the sixth form. Their essential feature is the introduction of *half-subjects* at the Advanced Level of the G.C.E. A half-subject would contain fifty per cent of the factual content of a specialist subject. If we assume an approximate reduction of present A-level syllabuses by twenty-five per cent than a half-subject would contain about three-eighths of the factual content of a present A-level syllabus. A half-subject would be taken in exactly the same way as a full A-level after two years in the sixth form. But the papers examining half-subjects are what would be called the *Complementary Level* of the G.C.E. (G.C.E., C-level). Success in these papers could then be used in two ways: by the A-level candidates for whom it would be counted as a half-subject at A-level; by the non

A-level candidate for whom it would be counted as a pass at Complementary Level. Thus we have an examination sufficiently flexible to meet the needs of a much wider range of ability in the sixth form.

In Diagram 4 we have illustrated a possible sixth-form course for the non-A-level candidate which would be examined at Complementary Level. This course provides for a spread of five or six subjects and it offers the child some choice of subjects. We see no reason why all the subjects need be taken simultaneously throughout the two years in the sixth form, although they would be examined simultaneously at the end of the sixth-form course. For example it would probably be a good thing to allow more time in the first year for 'reading' in the language and literature courses and for the essential groundwork in economics or statistics, whereas the second year would be the best time for the study of the Impact of Science on Modern Life and Thought. On the other hand the courses on art and music appreciation might very well run for three or four periods throughout both years. Obviously the timetabling would depend on the qualifications of teachers in the different schools. But the non-A-level candidate would find in this curriculum a really stimulating sixth-form course which would provide him with a first-rate educational background.

For the A-level candidate the advantages are no less obvious. Diagram 2 shows the new-type curriculum to which we have already referred in our discussion of the basic curriculum for secondary schools. In the new-type curriculum A-level would contain two and a half *specialist* and one and a half *coherence* subjects. The specialist subjects would occupy about half the total teaching time and would be taught and examined on the present A-level pattern with a twenty-five-per-cent reduction of factual content. The coherence subjects, for which new syllabuses will be required, would be taught and examined at the new Complementary Level. These subjects would be taken together by all sixth-formers, according to year rather than ability; for ten or eleven periods a week therefore both A-level and C-level candidates would be taught together. The resulting

Diagram 4 *Non-A-level Sixth-Form Course to be examined at C-level*

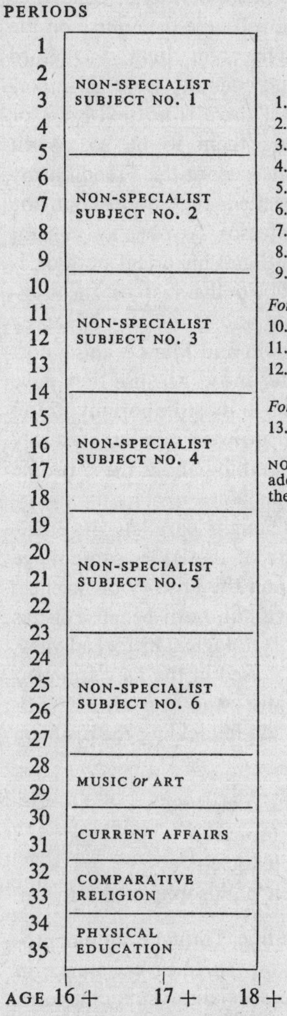

PERIODS	
1	
2	
3	NON-SPECIALIST SUBJECT NO. 1
4	
5	
6	
7	NON-SPECIALIST SUBJECT NO. 2
8	
9	
10	
11	
12	NON-SPECIALIST SUBJECT NO. 3
13	
14	
15	
16	NON-SPECIALIST SUBJECT NO. 4
17	
18	
19	
20	
21	NON-SPECIALIST SUBJECT NO. 5
22	
23	
24	
25	NON-SPECIALIST SUBJECT NO. 6
26	
27	
28	
29	MUSIC *or* ART
30	
31	CURRENT AFFAIRS
32	COMPARATIVE
33	RELIGION
34	PHYSICAL
35	EDUCATION

AGE 16+ 17+ 18+

NON-SPECIALIST SUBJECTS:

1. Use of English language and literature
2. Social studies (history and geography)
3. Political studies (economics and government)
4. Commercial or statistical mathematics
5. Impact of science on modern life and thought
6. Modern language and European culture
7. Music appreciation
8. Art
9. Religious knowledge

For girls only

10. Domestic science
11. Pre-nursing
12. Secretarial studies

For boys only

13. Industrial arts

NOTE. The C-level papers listed above are in addition to those 'coherence subjects' required in the '2½ + 1½' A-level scheme listed in Diagram 2.

examination would, however, provide. A-level candidates with a half-subject at A-level.

What do we aim to achieve by the introduction of coherence subjects? Every candidate at A-level will take the course on the Development of Scientific Thought. Not long ago Lord Cherwell suggested that Faraday and Fleming were as important as Walpole and Wellington. But there is no text-book or examination syllabus that considers them to be so. When Napoleon landed in Egypt in 1798 it was not the French army but the French scientists who excited the interest of the Egyptians. It is difficult to resist Professor Toynbee's comment that 'this antediluvian Western traditional historical outlook is not going to last much longer'.[69] To the rest of the non-Western world Faraday and Fleming and Galileo and Harvey and Voltaire and Rousseau and Darwin and Marx – and a host of others – are the people who matter most, because they gave birth to the modern world. If the single most important strand in modern society is the story of the European mind, then surely we can insist that children know something about these people and their ideas.

The Development of Scientific Thought parallels the Intellectual History that is now a feature of the American college curriculum. It is an improvement upon the History of Science. The History of Science has remained still-born because it has been based too carefully upon the chronological historical view. The sequences of scientific discovery used in the Development of Scientific Thought should first satisfy the four aims identified by the Science Masters' Association in tackling the problem of numeracy for the arts specialist.

1. Provide an introduction to 'scientific method'.
2. Develop five or six fundamental topics.
3. Illustrate the impact of science on society.
4. Illustrate the impact of science on philosophy and religion.

Secondly the Development of Scientific Thought should provide a broadening of background knowledge or coherence in the study of science for the science specialist. This course of study, together with physical education, current affairs, religion, and music or art, would become the common element in the sixth-form curriculum.

The 'scientific case histories' used on this course will have to be chosen with some care, but Newtonian Physics, Atomic Theory, Darwinian Evolution, and the Number Field are examples of what we have in mind; each based on observation, each tested and modified, each covering a different topic, and each having a profound influence on the modern world.

The sixth-former who is also a university candidate will thus be taking two and a half specialist subjects and one and a half coherence subjects: that is, two specialist subjects at A-level and one specialist subject at C-level, together with three other non-specialist subjects at C-level, one of which will be the Development of Scientific Thought. The arts child will choose a second coherence subject from either English, history, or a modern language, remembering that the subject selected must be different from the specialist subjects chosen: the third coherence subject chosen will be either mathematics or statistics. The science child will have English or history for his second coherence subject and a choice of modern language for the third subject.

In Diagrams 2 and 4 we have summarized what at first sight may appear to be a rather complicated scheme. We must repeat that 'two and a half and one and a half', together with a total of seven periods spent on physical education, current affairs, religion, and music or art, is the *full* sixth-form course designed for the intending university entrant; we recognize that the less able child will not be able to cope with this sort of timetable and we put forward a timetable based on a choice of six C-level subjects, to be examined after two years in the sixth form, and list a number of alternatives in Diagram 4.

For all *coherence* courses new syllabuses are required. It would be utterly disastrous if existing A-level syllabuses were merely to be truncated; this could not possibly meet the demands of the new sixth-form curriculum. These syllabuses should be drawn up by joint panels of school teachers and university teachers.

On 9 April 1961 the following resolution was sent to the Joint Four,* the National Union of Teachers, and the National Association of Schoolmasters:

> At three conferences on the sixth-form curriculum arranged at Oxford by the University Department of Education, and attended by 96 heads of schools and 128 assistant masters and mistresses, there was strong support for the introduction of half-subjects into the structure of the G.C.E. Advanced Level examination.(39)
>
> Of the three alternatives for the adaption of the sixth-form curriculum to modern needs – the Peterson proposals for specialist arts and sciences at A-level, the proposal for the introduction of examinable general studies at A-level, and the introduction of half-subjects at C-level – we believe that the introduction of half-subjects would be the best basis for the future of sixth-form education.

Atmosphere and speciality – these are the qualities which should govern the sixth form. Inevitably we have been concerned with the organization of knowledge. But this is not enough. There must be time for children to learn to appreciate and enjoy a cultural life. The need for cultural appreciation is just as important as the need to speak good English or learn mathematics. Five or six periods a week should be devoted to the cultural subjects which we have broadly defined as art, music, religion, and current affairs. These subjects are not susceptible to the technique of classroom teaching. Often they will involve lectures by outside people, by actors or architects or politicians, for instance; or they may require visits to concerts or the theatre or the cinema. These things cannot always be fitted in advance into school timetables. All we require is that they should be recognized, not as peripheral activities to be indulged in when the 'serious' work of the classroom has been finished, but as an essential part of sixth-form education.

* The Joint Committee of the four Secondary Associations, popularly known as 'the Joint Four'.

Concerned with the future of the nation of which I am a member and working overseas for the past fourteen months, I have been interested to observe the many pages of finely laid-out advertisements for employment in what are called our 'quality' daily and Sunday newspapers.

I have yet to see one single advertisement for a composer, musician, painter, sculptor, architect, playwright, novelist, poet, actor, or film director – all of whom surely will be the creative influence in our culture in the next ten, twenty-five, or fifty years to come. If we have any culture left.[59]

Some prophets have predicted that if we escape the Orwellian world we may nevertheless emerge as a society devoted to a 'kindly materialism'. A people stuffed with knowledge, but a people whose brains have atrophied. An ordered bureaucracy in which the venturesome receive penalties rather than rewards. A soothing, insular, pastoral scene. It is not yet too late to confound the prophets.

Trained intelligence, as Professor Whitehead once reminded us, is the condition of survival in this century. This we have now accepted and at long last, at the eleventh hour, we have begun to give the British people the educational system they deserve. But Lord Radcliffe noted a characteristic of our race which may yet prevent the achievement of this system:

The British [he said] have formed the habit of praising their institutions, which are sometimes inept, and of ignoring the character of their race, which is often superb. In the end they will be in danger of losing their character and being left with their institutions: a result disastrous indeed.[43]

Nowhere is this more true than over the question of the reform of the sixth-form curriculum. The English sixth form has received so much praise in the past that it has been endowed with qualities which, although often absent today, make it sacrosanct to the reformer. What is needed is the widest possible discussion of the sixth-form curriculum followed by action on the part of both the universities and the schools. This we regard as a matter of urgency if we are to ensure intellectual survival.

CHAPTER 7

The School Examination System

WHICH came first? The examinations or the schools? Do boys go to secondary schools in order to pass examinations? Will Johnny pass his 11-plus? What position will Johnny get in the class after the end-of-term examinations? Will Johnny get through his G.C.E.? Will Johnny get two A-levels? Will Johnny get a university place? Is it all a giant hurdle-race with the hurdles getting higher all the time?

Or is it just an industry? *An Introduction to Chemistry at Ordinary Level* by an Assistant Examiner in Chemistry at the General Certificate of Education. Or, *English for Schools* – 'eminently suitable for candidates preparing for G.C.E. at O-level'. Or, *New Records for the G.C.E.*, 'for list of other records for these examinations apply, quoting "G.C.E." to ...' What are they studying? Is it a new subject called G.C.E.?

Or is it because teachers don't have anything else to say? A headmaster: 'I can say for all subjects that the teaching is bounded by the O-level syllabus.' Or an English master: 'I direct the study of the set books almost entirely in accordance with the questions which have been asked on them in the past.' Or the head of a grammar-school department: 'We do hug our chains, don't we?'

Whatever the reason may be, it is true that external examinations, of which the General Certificate of Examination is the best known, have assumed great importance in secondary schools. It is true for example that these examinations are, in the minds of a large number of parents, the *raison d'être* of the school. It is also true that there are a number of headmasters and headmistresses, as well as assistant teachers, who today regard the passing of external examinations as the chief aim of their schools. It is true that the competitive nature of the pass mark in these examinations has had an adverse and a narrowing effect upon teaching syllabuses. And finally, although this can scarcely be proven, it is true that examination pressure now bears much more heavily upon children than it has done in the past.

Now, very few people would wish for an education system which abolished external examinations; neither for that matter would the majority of teachers! For one thing the public likes to feel that there is a concrete achievement in exchange for the money which it spends on education. Employers have need of an assessment by which they can judge the school-leaver applying for his first job. The child himself needs the incentive of an examination to take him along a severe course of study. And even the teacher, as he plies his trade, is sometimes grateful for the fact of an external examination towards which he can get his class to work. The interested parties all want to have external examinations. Why do they complain then? It is not abolition they want, but reform.

It is, we understand, a cardinal principle of the Ministry of Education that examinations must *follow and not determine* the curriculum of the school. If this principle were to be followed – it is not at the moment – many of the difficulties would fall into perspective. We believe that the widespread criticism of the examination system at the present time is both fair and justified and that it results from the failure to try to apply this principle. The reforms we propose would, we think, go a long way towards implementing the Ministry's theory.

First, what is the purpose, not of examinations in general, but of each particular examination? Clearly there are two types: some, such as the 11-plus, are predictive tests, designed to ascertain capacity; others, such as most of the examinations taken by secondary-school children, are attainment tests, designed to assess knowledge acquired. Leaving aside for the moment the predictive type of examination, let us look at the General Certificate of Education, which is the prototype of all the others.

The General Certificate at Ordinary Level is a qualifying examination to test that a certain amount of knowledge has been acquired. The most striking thing we notice immediately about it is that in 1959, the last record at the time of writing, only 58·5 per cent of all the candidates who sat in each subject passed the examination. Why this wretchedly low standard of achievement for this type of examination? Is the answer that the examiners did not intend to pass more than 58·5 per cent of the candidates whatever the standard achieved in the examination? (They passed 58·7 per cent in 1958!) It is the policy of examining boards that a little under half of those who sit for the principal secondary-school examination shall inevitably fail. This is a curious policy when we reflect that this examination is a qualifying one testing four years of secondary-school work; it is in no sense a competitive examination governing selection of a small number of boys for a few treasured places at the university or anything like that. It is curious because it is in the nature of a qualifying examination that the vast majority should pass while only a tiny minority fail. Clearly this is not happening with the General Certificate at Ordinary Level.

What is the effect of this policy upon the schools, where it is known that only fifty-eight per cent of candidates in each subject will pass the examination? Teachers are under pressure from both parents and nowadays even the children themselves ('Please, sir, we're not interested in that because it's not in the syllabus') to make sure that they are not among the unfortunate forty-two per cent. And so the teachers stick closer and closer to the examination syllabus, and the non-examinable but often the most educative of all the subjects get less time in the timetable as the examination approaches. At the same time the teachers have an ever-decreasing desire or incentive to try new aspects of their subject or even suggest new topics for inclusion in the official syllabus. This is proved by the fact that teachers make little use of the standing offer by all the examining boards to present their own syllabuses, connected, for example, with the peculiar locale of their school, for approval as examinable topics. And so the deadly apathy of bureaucracy descends upon teaching until we get, as Mr Peterson reminds us, the master at one school who had taken the form through the *Medea* every Christmas term for the last twenty years until the text-books themselves which the boys used were actually scored with the volume of applause considered fitting by previous generations for each one of the master's preordained little jokes. Scarcely a way of communicating enthusiasm to young minds!

The remedy we suggest is a simple one. Instead of the examining boards declaring that they will pass fifty-eight per cent of all candidates, they should declare that they will pass eighty per cent. This means that four out of five of those who sit the examination will pass it. This will make it a proper qualifying examination, passing the great majority and eliminating only the minority who will be sub-standard. It amounts to a declaration that if a child has studied hard for the sort of examination which is within his range of capabilities he stands a very good chance of qualifying in that subject. The examination will become one that children can take in their stride, requiring hard work and a good standard of achievement, but not something for which they have to be crammed to the exclusion of all the rest of education. With the new pass-mark a great deal of the examination tension will be removed from both the parents and the child's point of view. The examination will therefore achieve the Ministry's aim of following rather than determining the work of the school.

At this point we can hear the familiar cry of 'standards'. We can see absolutely no argument whatever to prove that the maintenance of academic standards necessitates the failure of nearly half of all examination candidates. All that is proved by this heavy failure-rate is that the examination is not fulfilling the qualifying purpose for which it was set; or that some of the candidates were too weak to enter for this particular examination; or that, as is certainly the case with French, a new type of paper is urgently needed. Academic standards are not maintained by setting an examination paper and then deliberately ensuring that so many fail. Certainly new papers may be needed in order to raise the number of passes, but these papers will inevitably be set more within the range of the majority of children. This is exactly what should be done. At the same time we think it would be a good thing under the new system to register failures as well as passes on a child's record. A subject would not lightly be undertaken if a boy knew that failure had important consequences. From the psychological point of view the new system could do nothing but good for the candidate; from the teacher's point of view, he would not find that a truly qualifying examination would impede the natural process of his teaching. The examination would return to its rightful position as one of the aids towards effective education.

What would be the effect of the higher pass-rate on the placing of school-leavers in jobs? (We shall consider the question of university selection later on in Chapter 8.) One of our large firms, J. and P. Coats Ltd, has this to say: 'Candidates with three or four G.C.E. O-level passes will be considered. Standards are not absolute and much attention is paid to personal qualities.' [13] The General Certificate of Education is not designed to predict, and it is clearly incapable of predicting with much accuracy, what a boy or girl will achieve during the first five years of his working life. Our history is crammed full of the stories of men and women who failed miserably under school conditions, only to reach pinnacles of achievement under the more normal conditions of the ordinary world. From the examination system the employer wishes to know that he will be taking on boys and girls who have successfully absorbed a first-rate general education and who have reached the maturity expected of them. This is the kind of foundation on which he can build the training course for his particular firm. What he requires is, above all, a really thorough leaving certificate. In this certificate the G.C.E. will certainly play an important part.

The establishment of the General Certificate of Education as a qualifying examination with a high pass-rate which can be taken by the majority of children in their stride will require certain important reforms in our present procedure. In the first place a good deal of experiment will have to go into syllabuses in order to ensure that they really are in accord with the pattern of education which the teachers consider right for the child. Under the present system, G.C.E. passes are awarded by some boards at the ridiculously low mark of forty per cent, and in order to prevent too many children passing, the examining boards are always under the temptation to insert the esoteric question calculated to unseat all but the minority of candidates who have very often been lucky enough to have been taught by a teacher who is an 'ace' spotter of examination questions. The contest in fact has become one between the board and the teacher, with the child as mere cannon-fodder. But in a 'qualifying' examination it will be reasonable to expect a pass-mark in the region of seventy per cent, for 'qualifying' in a subject will mean that the candidate has absorbed effectively most of what he has been taught. And this surely is the whole point of teaching for such an examination. For obvious reasons, when gun-drill is taught in the Royal Navy personnel are not permitted to pass out knowing less than half of what they have been taught. Why therefore should we permit candidates to pass an important academic test when the marks show that they have absorbed less than half of the subject matter?

In order to bring the syllabus more into line with the teaching that children have received in schools, one important principle must be established in the composition of the examining boards. On all boards the majority should in future be from the schools themselves. It is entirely reasonable to insist that, on any board that is determining syllabuses and setting examination papers for the Ordinary Level of the General Certificate, two-thirds of the board should consist of those who work in schools, head teachers and assistant teachers. The remaining third should be composed of university teachers and perhaps representatives of industry and the professions. The representatives of the universities, industry, and the professions should not be there to impose policy upon the schools, but to advise on policy that has been determined by the schools themselves. Just as it is eminently sensible to allow the universities and the professions to decide the type of examination on which they will award first degrees and professional qualifications, so it is equally sound to allow the teachers themselves to decide the type of examination that will be taken at the end of the main secondary-school course. Since 1857, when Oxford University agreed to conduct extra-mural examinations for the first time, the historical trend has been to increase the role of the universities on examination boards. The creation of the Secondary Schools Examination Council at the end of the First World War, and even the creation of the special subject panels, has not reversed this trend. Only a change of majority on the boards themselves can provide really suitable examinations for the schools.

What kind of syllabuses and examinations might result from these reforms? There would be a great change in the role of examinations in secondary schools. The nature of a true 'qualifying' examination in which both the pass-mark and the pass-rate would be considerably higher would prevent the General Certificate from dominating the curriculum. It would become much more like an internal examination with outside assessment and would be something taken quite normally by children at the end of the first part of their school careers. The curriculum would in consequence be broadened because it would no longer be necessary to develop such concentration on the 'examination' subjects as to exclude the 'non-examination' subjects and activities. The 'non-examination' subjects, drama for example, would gain in prestige and authority. The newly composed examination boards would, we think, be more competent to provide suitable syllabuses for the schools. By their constitution they should be required to revise the whole of their syllabuses at regular intervals. There would also be more incentive for schools to submit their own syllabuses to these boards, a right which they now have in theory but rarely exercise. With the increasing strain of examination pressure taken off both children and teachers, better education would develop.

We wish to apply to the whole examination system principles we have discussed with particular reference to the Ordinary Level of the General Certificate of Education:

1. An examination exists to serve the needs of the children at varying stages of their education and to provide employers and the public with satisfying evidence that this education has been efficiently carried out.
2. A *qualifying* examination should be set at a standard at which about four-fifths of the candidates will qualify. In order to prevent children being entered for unsuitable examinations failures will be noted on their Leaving Certificates.
3. Such a qualifying examination can be set only by examining boards which have a majority of teacher members who will be assisted and advised by university, professional, and industrial bodies.
4. To ensure that syllabuses are kept up to date, all examining boards must be compelled to revise completely their syllabuses at intervals of not more than five years.
5. Schools and individual teachers should be given a good deal of encouragement to submit their own syllabuses for consideration to the examining boards.

The application of these principles will lead to the creation of new examinations to meet new needs. We envisage (see Diagram 5, page 156) that there will be four examinations levels in secondary schools. The Ordinary Level of the G.C.E. we have already discussed. As we deplore the present tendency to use the Ordinary Level for children in all types of schools, for many of whom a less literary type of examination would be suitable, we endorse the Report of the Beloe Committee* that there should be 'examinations designed to suit candidates of a reasonably high competence and ability at a level somewhat below that of G.C.E. O-level'.[47] The Beloe examinations will, we hope, play a major part in raising educational achievement in the non-selective schools. There are three main principles behind the Beloe proposals: first, that these examinations 'should

* A committee of the Secondary School Examinations Council (S.S.E.C.), which was set up to study the question of examinations other than the G.C.E. in secondary schools.

Diagram 5 *Four Examination Levels*

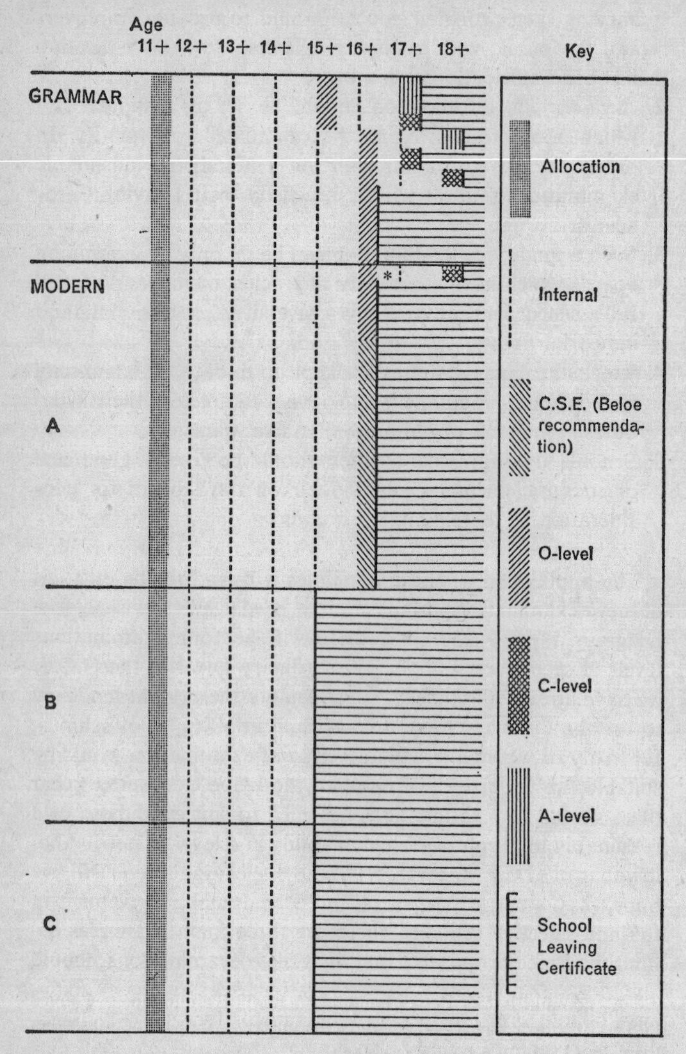

* Transferred to grammar school sixth form

be specially designed to suit the needs and interests of pupils in the ability range concerned and should not simply provide a replica of G.C.E. examinations at a lower level';[47] secondly, that these examinations 'should be largely in the hands of teachers serving in the schools which will use them';[47] thirdly, that they should be conducted by new examining boards set up on a regional basis and staffed by 'representatives of teachers serving in the region, local education authorities, further education institutions, area training organizations, and employers'.[47]

With the Beloe proposals there is an excellent chance to take a really decisive step forward in the education of children in the upper streams of secondary modern schools and the lower streams of grammar schools. In recent years the pattern has too often been that, in their attempts to get G.C.E. O-level, for which in most subjects they are not suited, their general education has been sacrificed. Long hours of work have resulted in a single pass: the enthusiasm of both child and teacher has been killed. In any case from the practical viewpoint it is undesirable to increase the strain on the existing nine G.C.E. examining boards. Therefore Beloe, with its new examining boards, its teacher participation, and its new type of examination will have much influence on the future of these schools. All that is needed is that the new examining bodies should recruit to their ranks at this vital stage some really able men and women. We suggest not only that local education authorities should 'make a positive contribution by encouraging and helping teachers to do this work', [47] but also that examiners should be paid good fees.

What is the purpose of examinations in the sixth form? The examinations at this stage fulfil a twofold objective. On the one hand there is the Advanced Level of the G.C.E. which has now very largely taken the place of the old matriculation requirements of the universities. The A-level examination, therefore, is a qualifying examination which tests a two-year sixth-form course with the specific intention of deciding whether a child is capable of going on to higher education. We shall discuss the A-level more fully in connexion with the problem of university selection (see Chapter 8).

On the other hand there are many children who do not require A-level. There are some who stay in the sixth form for only a year and then leave to follow a career for which A-level passes are unnecessary. There are others who wish to pursue a sixth-form course but who have not the ability to reach A-level. In particular there are many girls in the sixth forms of girls' schools for whom the specialization of A-level is unsuitable. For all these, the present A-level is unsatisfactory because its standards and its degree of specialization compel them to abandon the general education which they require.

To meet the needs of these children there should be the new Complementary Level of the G.C.E. which would be suitable for non-A-level sixth-formers, and to which we have already referred (see page 141). The C-level paper would either be taken as a sixth-form leaving examination or, as we have indicated, it could be taken as a half-subject complementing G.C.E. A-level. The introduction of this new level, with a factual content approximately equivalent to three-eighths of our present A-level examination, will require new syllabuses and new examination papers. We envisage that these syllabuses will incorporate the best parts of the existing Alternative Ordinary Level of the G.C.E. as well as much that is entirely new. The construction of these new syllabuses and examination papers should be one of the first tasks of the reformed examination boards.

The principles which we have applied to the Ordinary Level of the G.C.E. should be applied to C-level, namely that it should be a *qualifying* examination. We should expect that approximately eighty per cent of candidates who have taken a serious sixth-form course should pass at C-level. The effect of establishing C-level as a *qualifying* examination for the non-A-level sixth-former should be to relax sixth-form pressure and enable a much broader general education to take place. By setting an eighty-per-cent pass-rate and recording failures on C-level certificates we should be setting a target that many more sixth-formers could aim at. At the same time we should abolish the present practice of the less able sixth-former repeating his A-level work for the sole reason of getting a few more marks. This practice is the negation of true sixth-form education.

The introduction of two new levels of examinations in secondary schools – the Beloe examinations and C-level of the General Certificate of Education – combined with raising both the pass mark and the percentage pass rate of all candidates entering for any of these examinations, should react favourably upon the vexed question of the 11-plus examination. Under this system the non-selective schools will have their own targets to aim at, instead of striving after examinations that are only suitable for grammar schools. Contrary to general opinion, children for the most part assess their own capabilities realistically. Faced with a standard of achievement that is fundamentally beyond them, their work gets worse and not better. It is simply not true to argue that the cause of education is served by maintaining a rigid level in the examination system and trying to drag all children up to such a level.

In 1944 Mr J. L. Brereton wrote that it was 'the Board of Education's cardinal principle that the examinations must follow and not determine the curriculum'.(7) This is the principle that we wish to apply. By introducing new levels and by using the examinations as qualifying examinations in which we expect the majority of candidates to pass, we consider this principle can be achieved. We shall have a flexible examination system which will be the servant and not the master of education.

CHAPTER 8

The Problem of University Selection

In 1960 there were some 108,000 students in the English and Welsh universities; this is twice the university population of 1939. By 1965 there will be about 136,000; by 1970 this number will rise towards 170,000. Thus in a period of thirty years the number of university students in England and Wales will have almost quadrupled. But reference to other countries (see Table 1, page 29) will show that even this expansion will not be particularly striking. Our concern here, however, is not with university education but with the problems of selecting university students. Clearly a great deal will depend on the selection of these men and women. Economically, a single university place costs not less than £700 a year, twelve times the cost of a secondary-school place. Bad selection will be expensive. Nationally we have to ensure that there are a sufficient number of qualified men and women to undertake the increasingly complicated task of guiding our modern society. And from the human point of view we believe – and this can be neither proved nor disproved – that the massive expansion of sixth forms in secondary schools in recent years has shown that many more boys and girls than formerly are now capable of profiting from university education. For all these reasons it is imperative that we evolve an efficient system by which we can select university students.

But we cannot select boys and girls for universities unless we have a good idea of the type of education for which we are selecting them. Thirty years ago our universities were composed of the boys (and a very few girls) who had gained awards from the grammar schools, fighting their way up the educational ladder by sheer academic ability, and of boys, many of them from the public schools, who were intellectually competent rather than outstanding, and whose parents paid for their university education. On graduation one of two courses was usually followed: the brilliant who had read and succeeded in taking high Honours Degrees went rapidly to the top of their respective professions, thus providing concrete evidence of the well-known fact that English universities provide first-rate education for first-rate intellects; the rest, academically mediocre, had received a social education which entitled them to fit very nicely into some corner of what in England is commonly referred to as 'the establishment'. Unfortunately this cosy state of affairs, essentially a hangover from the nineteenth century, when a small élite was considered all that was necessary for the wealth and happiness of England, has been completely shattered in the last twenty years. It is now clear that we need a massive expansion in the numbers receiving university education in this country, coupled with a re-thinking of the content of university education itself.

But it takes more than a war to change long-established ideas in England. And the idea of the university catering for an élite and only an élite has waxed strong in the post-war years. In fact it has had profound effects on the whole structure of secondary education. Such a university education means reading for an Honours Degree, with the consequent denigration of the General or Pass Degree. It means depth rather than breadth; and depth to the exclusion of breadth has forced sixth forms into excessive specialization in order to meet the entrance requirements of universities. It has accentuated the imbalance between Oxbridge, traditionally the élite universities, and Redbrick who cater, in the words of an alderman from a provincial university town, for 'the throw-outs of better places'. And, since the war, universities have come to select their students more and more on academic merit as determined by examination marks. Élite education has imposed such severe strains on the student that the current failure-rate in British universities runs at about fifteen per cent of all students and about twenty per cent of students in Honours schools.

Now what will be the characteristics of the expanding university courses of the future? Clearly the specialized Honours course will remain the best possible training for the highly intelligent student, the 'high-fliers' of secondary schools who will be needed in increasing numbers in posts of pure research in all branches of knowledge. These people will continue to set the standards of the professions and they will be in continuous demand in the industrial and administrative worlds. Many more of them will go on to post-graduate work to play an increasing part in the intellectual basis of our society. Their role will be of cardinal importance, as in the past. But it is now becoming equally clear that we shall need very much larger numbers of really well-educated people who are just below the first rank in intelligence: technologists to support the scientists, teachers to support the professors, executives to support the administrators, social workers to support the sociologists. For most of these professional people a broad degree course will be the best equipment for the job. One such degree course, as we suggest in Chapter 10, should be the Degree in Education. At Keele such courses have already been developed and plans are being discussed at the other new universities. 'We need lots more higher education, but not lots more Honours Degree courses – such is the text upon which a number of us are working and thinking.'[(59)] We agree.

What principles of selection would ensure that the expanding universities of the future will get the right type of person for higher education? First, the 'high-flier', the exceptionally intelligent boy or girl. His route to the university today has often been compared to the racing stable. Selected by the 11-plus, he enters the grammar school where he is put into the A-stream with the other 'high-fliers'. For reasons which have never been made quite clear, he is immediately brought 'under pressure'. The reasons have not been clarified, because when he emerges at the university the complaint is then made that he has been under such pressure, which means such concentration on his specialized subjects, that he has already very often covered the first year of the Honours course and has, at the university, to mark time. However, he is kept under intensive grammar-school pressure, and because of the feeling that above all he must have 'examination security' he proceeds at fifteen-plus to amass a series of high marks at G.C.E. O-level. Two years later 'he feels the pressure of having to get the fifty-five or sixty per cent at his A-level'.(32) But A-level is only the preliminary to the university scholarship examinations, the pinnacle of which is an award at Oxford or Cambridge and an appearance in *The Times*. Finally the 'high-flier' clears the last fence and reaches the university.

He has been selected for the university, but a more important question remains – has he been given the sort of preparation that will enable him to make the best use of his university education? Let us look at the less intelligent sixth-formers who will in the future, as university education expands, make up the increasing numbers of applicants for university places. The 'high-flier' may well survive the racing stable – although the fact that there is a higher failure-rate for students in Honours schools indicates that he may not be altogether immune – but the less intelligent sixth-former will suffer from this system. He is not intelligent enough to gain a scholarship to the university. Therefore he knows that his place will depend upon his A-level marks. What does he do? More and more of his time in the sixth-form years goes into preparing for this examination which alone can guarantee him a place. Between the ages of sixteen and eighteen he is compelled to concentrate exclusively upon A-level papers because he has 'that awful sense that he's got to get five more marks at the A-level'.(32) The ultimate idiocy is reached when he is informed that he must repeat the A-level course in order to take the examination again and gain the necessary extra marks. The effect of such over-concentration in the sixth form upon the less intelligent boy is the opposite of the sort of education which he should be receiving at that age. What will be required of him when he starts to read for a broad degree will be a sound basic general education. This is precisely what he cannot receive when more and more of his time is being given to preparation for A-level in his specialized subjects.

What type of minds do we want when boys and girls embark upon university education? In 1932 Professor Whitehead wrote:

> Speaking generally, during the last thirty years the schools of England have been sending up to the universities a disheartened crowd of young folk, inoculated against any outbreak of intellectual zeal.(74)

Now, thirty years later, we have embarked upon a momentous experiment in secondary and higher education. Can we create the conditions – for we do not think they exist at the moment – whereby we can send up to the universities crowds of ebullient young people with an imaginative zest for intellectual life?

Our proposals for the sixth form, which are based upon the suggested introduction of half-subjects at G.C.E. A-level and the establishment of a non-specialized course at G.C.E. C-level, are designed to re-establish the coherence of sixth-form education; that is, to make sixth-form education once again the best intellectual training available to boys and girls in their late teens 'without reckoning on any extension or completion of it later on'. This concept of the sixth form will be ruined if the present anxiety about getting a place at the university is not allayed. If these boys and girls are to arrive at the university full of imaginative intellectual energy, sixth-form education must not take place in an atmosphere of worry and fear about the future.

The only way to prevent such anxiety is to establish a fair standard of academic achievement and make it quite plain that on reaching this standard a sixth-former will have *qualified* for a university place. This is the maximum amount of worry that it is reasonable to impose on the sixth-former. In plain terms this means that a child of eighteen will know that, provided he reaches the necessary examination standard, he will be guaranteed a place in a university. His job will be to reach the required standard; it will be our job to arrange for his *selection* to a particular university.

On 12 May 1961 the Minister of Education announced changes in the Advanced Level of the General Certificate of Education examination, designed to ensure 'that the examination will continue effectively to meet the needs of sixth forms while keeping "examination pressures" to the minimum compatible with the fair and orderly transition of sixth-form leavers to higher education, to professions or other employment'.[45] This reform, based upon the third report of the Secondary Schools Examination Council, is a compromise. The nine examining boards are to establish a uniform system of grading and presentation of results of the A-level examination. Numerical marks are to be abolished; it is hoped this will ensure that a candidate does not take the same paper for the second time merely to gain a few additional marks. The grading system will be a five-point one running from Grade A to Grade E. All A-level candidates will be placed in a grade on the results of examination in their specialist subjects. In addition to the basic papers in specialist subjects, there will be special or S-papers designed for the more able candidates. Any candidate who reaches Grade A, B, or C in the basic papers will then have this S-paper taken into consideration. But an essential feature of the reform is that the S-papers – and no candidate may present more than two S-papers – will be considered only if a candidate has first reached one of the higher basic grades. The reform, which is due to come in in 1963, is designed to achieve three things: first, that the examination pressure on the average sixth-former will be no more than a reasonable pressure; secondly, that the A-level examination will provide, with the aid of the S-papers, a reasonable standard of achievement for those who select boys and girls for the universities and professions; thirdly, that the assessment of the A-level examination will achieve parity throughout the country.

These changes in the Advanced Level of the G.C.E. are no more than an interim solution. Our proposals for the introduction of C-level for the weaker sixth-former, and for the introduction of half-subjects to complement the specialized subjects of the A-level candidate, both offer a real chance of providing examinations for different ranges of interest and ability. Not so the current changes. There is for instance no guarantee that under the new system of grades candidates will not go on repeating the papers (as they do at present) in order to get a higher grade. Furthermore, many sixth-form teachers are disturbed by the fact that the new system will abolish the present S-level general paper in favour of setting S-level papers based directly on the specialized A-level syllabus. The S-level candidate, in short, will sit a sort of super A-level paper for his university qualification. The effect of the system will be a further narrowing of the syllabus at the top end and could easily lead to more cramming in the sixth form. We cannot support the new system except as a compromise pending the more radical reforms which we have suggested.

We turn to the blue riband of university selection: the scholarship system and the university entrance scholarships awarded at Oxford and Cambridge. They were endowed by the Oxford and Cambridge colleges to provide university education for poor boys in the days when no alternative university education existed except for London and Manchester universities. The purpose of these scholarships, then as now, was to select the ablest pupils for Oxford and Cambridge. The scholarships have over the years brought up to Oxford and Cambridge a continuous supply of the most intelligent men and women in the country. The scholarships have attained considerable prestige, and many schools in fact are judged in the eyes of the public – and they wish to be so judged – by the number of awards which they gain at Oxford and Cambridge. What has been the effect of these scholarships on education?

Before the 1944 Act, when secondary education was available for only a small minority of English children and when the pressure on university places was almost non-existent, the scholarships continued to fulfil their original purpose – they selected the most intelligent children for Oxford and Cambridge. So relaxed were those far-off days that the candidate who just failed to get a scholarship usually had no difficulty in obtaining a place at the Oxbridge college of his choice without any further effort. Since 1944 the position has been almost reversed and the scholarships now do almost as much harm to education as once they did good. As there are ten or more candidates for each place at Oxbridge, as almost every parent, if truth were known, would like his child to go there, and as the prestige value of these scholarships is higher than ever before, a rat-race has developed. In the schools the rat-race takes the form of processing a child * for the Oxbridge scholarships. Very often he comes under pressure as a potential scholarship candidate long before he leaves the middle school. He may then be sent to a sixth form in which the school specializes in scholarship work almost irrespective of his own choice in the matter. In that sixth form he will be taught by a teacher with long experience of the necessary academic manoeuvres which must precede the attempt. And finally he sits for the scholarship. He has been prepared for the highest hurdle – but has he been educated?

There are two points which we must make. First, the child himself. The school has a responsibility towards each child, which is to help to place him on the next rung of the ladder after he leaves school. It is irresponsible to try to place him on the wrong rung on account of such influences as heavy parental pressure or the prestige of the school. Every school exists to serve the children in it; not the other way round. It is no service at all to a child to try to send him where he does not belong. Secondly, the interests of society. We believe we are now committed to a society of equitable educational opportunity. Oxford and Cambridge should be open to the best potential men and women that we have and we should try as far as possible to eliminate unfair advantage in the selection of candidates. We consider that the university scholarships, as at present constituted, amount to unfair advantage.

If all university scholarships were awarded after the first year at the university, when equal conditions had been ex-

* This particular rat-race is mainly a 'male' one owing to the disparity of the sexes at Oxbridge.

perienced by everybody, the awards would be of far more educational value. The disadvantages to the child of sixth-form cramming would be eliminated and yet another obstacle in the way of the general education of the sixth-former would have gone. At the same time the awards would go to the candidates who displayed the highest potential for university work, which is where the awards should be going but cannot go under present conditions. And if a by-product of the new scheme were to spread a little wider over the many other universities the talents and abilities of our best men and women, this, we think, would be an advantage for the educational standards of the country.

Our candidate has *qualified*: how is he to be *selected*? Until 1963 selection may still be conducted on the present system, which in the opinion of many teachers has already become anarchic. What happens? To begin with the child, while in the fifth form, makes a choice of his A-level subjects. This choice however must be made with more than one eye on the entrance requirements of more than one university, because there are few, very few, so confident that they will gamble all on a single choice. Now whereas each university will accept roughly the same A-level standard in the main subjects, all vary to a considerable extent in their requirements in supporting subjects. The most notorious variation was that which existed until recently in the requirement by Oxford and Cambridge of Latin to Ordinary Level. But the position in geography is much worse. Some universities regard it as an arts subject and require supporting Advanced Level passes in other arts subjects, while others treat it as a science with corresponding demands. What is the candidate to do if he plumps for geography as an art and fails to get a place at the university? It is much too late to start learning to regard it as a science and to try the other group of universities. In the end, if he wants to study geography, he will probably aim for a university in the United States or the Commonwealth. But it seems a pity that English universities cannot have their fair share of able geographers. In practice, schools aim to provide the sixth-former with a sufficiently wide spread of supporting subjects to enable him to apply to a range of universities. But the point is made: the complexity of the different requirements for each university is so great that it burdens both child and teacher.

'Intelligence' has more or less been added as a new subject in primary school: perhaps 'university entrance' might be a new subject for secondary schools.[32]

What happens next?

I applied to eleven universities: Manchester, Birmingham, Reading, Leeds, Leicester, Southampton, Bristol, Exeter. I can't remember them all at the moment.[32]

The thing is a mad scramble in which an immense amount of extra form-filling is imposed upon sixth-form teachers and heads and an equal amount of additional strain and stress falls upon the child. This scramble is accentuated by the fact that Oxbridge, where the competition is by far the greatest, hold their scholarship examinations both in December and in March, thus necessitating a third year in the sixth form. But what does a candidate do if Redbrick offers him a place at the end of his second year? Does he accept it or does he reject it and try his luck in the third year at Oxbridge? The scramble reaches its height in the autumn when A-level results are published and 'boys and girls who have not been accepted will be frantically chasing universities, and universities chasing boys and girls, the cleverest ones'.[32] The tragedy of it all is, as Lord James has pointed out, that 'the less intelligent sixth-former wants to go to a university, and he doesn't mind fundamentally what university he gets into'.[32] Is it beyond our wits to devise a better system?

Only a few months ago Mr Bartlett of Exeter University put forward an excellent proposal for simplifying admission to English universities. The basis of the proposal is that as many universities as can agree to do so should accept applications from all candidates on a common entry form:

This form would indicate at the head of the front page all the universities participating in this method of selection, and would permit the applicant to list a number of universities in order of preference giving the faculty and course proposed at each. Another page would accommodate the headmaster's report given under the headings agreed by universities at the conference in 1958, and the remaining two pages would set out particulars of the candidate required by universities at present. No particular difficulty should be encountered by universities in reaching agreement on the information necessary for an applicant's case to be considered.(1)

What happens next? It is so simple that it is difficult to believe that it could not be put into effect in the immediate future. The candidate has been permitted to list three universities in his order of preference on the application form.* The completed form is sent to the university which is the candidate's first choice. The first-choice university can either accept or reject the candidate. If accepted the candidate is notified and his place is assured. If rejected the candidate is notified of his rejection and automatically the university forwards the form to the university which is the candidate's second choice. If his first choice therefore is unsuccessful the candidate will find himself being automatically considered by his second-choice university without any extra form-filling on the part of anybody – applicant or headmaster. And so on. If the candidate is rejected by all three universities of his choice his application goes to a clearing house from which he may be notified of a place at any university where there are still places available.†

* Mr Bartlett suggested that an applicant should be allowed to list 'six or seven' universities; there is not enough time to allow him to list so many.

† On 27 April 1962 it was announced to the Press that in October 1963 the Universities' Central Council for Admissions, which is supported by nearly all universities and unversity colleges with the regrettable exception of Oxbridge, will begin a scheme similar to the one we have suggested here. The aims of the Council are to get places for qualified applicants, to ease the task of university selectors, and to obtain statistics which are not at present available. It is hoped to achieve these aims without preventing the universities from being absolutely free to select their own undergraduates.

The advantages of such a system are obvious. From the applicant's point of view he is spared a lot of worry, because once he has decided on his three choices for a university the matter is taken out of his hands. From the headmaster's point of view he is spared a great deal of tedious duplicating of reports on each candidate; he can afford to put everything into the single application form, confident in the knowledge that he is doing the best for the child. From the point of view of the university authorities they know not only the degree of choice for their own university expressed by the candidate but also that the candidate whom they call for interview is not at the same time being interviewed by several other universities. Finally, from the point of view of secretarial staffs Mr Bartlett estimates that the scheme will reduce the total number of applications in circulation from 'perhaps 150,000–200,000 to 40,000–50,000; a number in fact not very greatly exceeding the actual number of university places available'.(1)

One important change in the school year would contribute to the smooth running of this selection system. The Easter term should be lengthened and both G.C.E. O-level and G.C.E. A-level should be taken at the end of this lengthened Easter term. What would be the advantages of putting forward the G.C.E. examinations by two to three months?

First, let us look at the A-level position if the examinations were to be put forward. The A-level course would be a full two-year course in the sixth form which would run from the beginning of one summer term to the end of the Easter term two years later. The A-level examinations would take place at the end of the Easter term. The university candidate's application form, including his A-level results, would probably begin circulating towards the end of May. By mid-June first-choice selections would have taken place; second-choice selections by mid-July; third-choice selections by mid-August; by September the clearing house would begin to operate. In short, by the middle of September university selection would be completed. Boys and girls could face the autumn of the year in which they leave school with their immediate future assured. We should abolish the frantic autumn scramble for places which characterizes the present system.

We believe that the present system is wasteful for another reason. The uncertainty of university selection at the moment is a main cause of many schools accepting the fact that a university place can be ensured only by a third year in the sixth form. From every point of view the extra year, which is at the moment often spent in doing A-level for the second time, would be far better spent by extending university courses to four years. The four-year university course is the practice of most European countries and of the United States. As the university places become available we hope that many will follow the example of Keele and provide a four-year course. Now if the A-level course is to be strictly a full two-year course, and no longer, we must provide a university selection system at the end of it that ensures that children know before they leave school what the future holds for them.

In fact the putting forward of the A-level examination will provide a sixth-form course that lasts for two full academic years and one term – the summer term after the completion of A-level. This extra term might have many advantages. First of all it would be the term in which university interviewing took place and sixth-formers would not have their A-level studies interrupted, as they are at the moment, by having to go away for interviews. Secondly, we think that this last term could be a most valuable term in which post-A-level general education could take place; the examination pressure would be off and we envisage that some really first-class cultural studies could be pursued. Nor do we discount the possibility that boys and girls who are not university candidates would be able to leave school in the spring when there is a good labour market. For these reasons we do not consider that the extra post-A-level term would be wasted.

The term gained at the end of the sixth-form course would be lost from the O-level course. Many teachers now find that the summer term examinations, conducted as they often are in unpleasantly hot conditions, do not give the best O-level results. In any case, we do not consider that the loss of one term in a long course such as O-level would have any effect upon the results. Administratively the putting forward of the O-level examinations would throw the burden of examination marking upon the teachers themselves during the Easter holidays. O-level papers would be taken at the end of the Easter term. From the point of view of the head it would be necessary for him to reorganize his lower sixth form during the Easter holidays in preparation for the start of new sixth-form courses in the summer term. The time available to do this would certainly be a week or two shorter than at present. But if O-level papers are taken at the end of the Easter term the results, if not the marks, could be in the hands of schools by the beginning of May, when the shortened summer term would begin. And one advantage would surely accrue: the head would be able to give even more attention than he can at the moment to the organization of his lower sixth because he would not have to bother at the same time about problems concerning the lower forms. These will move up as at present at the beginning of the autumn term.

Our proposals for university selection are closely linked to our proposals for the sixth form. The sixth-form course, whether it leads to A-level or to C-level, should be a two-year course leading on, we hope, to four years at the university. Once a boy or girl has qualified at one of these levels his selection should be as straightforward as we can make it while allowing to the candidate as much freedom of choice as is possible within the time available. We consider that university scholarships would assess potential university quality more effectively if they were taken after the first year at the university and not as entrance scholarships. We do not in any case consider that the university entrance scholarship is today a good influence upon the sixth form. The selection system we have outlined would work most effectively if it were linked to the putting forward of the G.C.E. A- and O-level examinations to the end of a lengthened Easter term. This in its turn would have considerable cultural and administrative advantages for schools. Like many other people we think that the time to introduce a new procedure for university selection is now, before the massive expansion in the universities which will take place over the next decade. Can we not act in order to make sure that these new universities, and the older ones as well, get the men and women of real quality and ability?

CHAPTER 9

The School Community

NEAR the end of his book, *Culture and Society, 1780–1950,*[75] Mr Raymond Williams poses the question of what kind of culture we may expect in this country as a result of the social evolution through which we are now passing. He distinguishes two interpretations of the idea of community: the idea of service and the idea of solidarity. The idea of service grew up during the nineteenth century in reaction to the anarchic individualism of the profit motive in industrialization. It has been expressed in the ethical standards that govern our professions, and our Public and Civil Services. It has been fostered by a long educational tradition amongst the English middle classes, for whom certain things, such as striking, 'just aren't done'. It has conferred great benefits on our society. On the other hand the idea of solidarity has also been immensely beneficial. It was developed by the English working classes under the harsh impact of industrialism. When Ernest Bevin used to refer to 'my people' he was referring not to his fellow Englishmen but to the members of the Transport and General Workers' Union. Solidarity made possible the practice of strike action and the treatment meted out to the blackleg amongst his fellow strikers. Solidarity accounted for the growth and massive support of English football teams. Political solidarity amongst the working classes was the original basis of the English Labour Party, to whom much of the social reform of this century is due.

The future of our culture depends upon how well we can reconcile these two ideas. In Whitehall and in the local council chambers, on the governing bodies of schools and hospitals, at the editorial desks of our newspapers, and in the boardrooms of the television and broadcasting authorities, sit the controllers of our community life. 'They' are in charge, 'they' spend our money; 'they' control the vast bureaucracy of our public life; 'they' are – please note – the public 'servants' who know best. By their own lights 'they' try to practise the idea of service. What more natural than that 'we' should be governed by 'them'? But 'we', in the process, have escaped from responsibility. 'We' are not over-impressed by appeals not to neglect the national interest, or to increase production – production for whom, if we merely pay heavier taxes? If 'we' get to the top, 'we' feel no particular obligation to the community which made it possible for us to get there. If 'we' remain at the bottom, why should 'we' be grateful for any assistance which 'they' may happen to grant us in order to endure unemployment? And, except every four or five years, 'we' are neither interested in 'how we are governed' nor in the much more exciting possibility of 'how we might govern ourselves'.

Service from the top – Lady Bountiful – and solidarity at the bottom – Alfred Doolittle – must surely now give way to the idea of *active mutual responsibility*. In a democratic society it would seem to be perfectly possible to promote such a social ethic without impairing the position of the able leader. Lord James is mistaken, surely, in thinking that John Stuart Mill said the last word on democracy:

> No government by a democracy ... either in its political acts or in the opinions, qualities, and tone of mind which it fosters, ever did or could rise above mediocrity, except in so far as the sovereign Many have let themselves be guided (which in their best times they always have done) by the counsels and influence of a more highly gifted and instructed One or Few.(26)

If you ask older children at a good school, particularly scientists, what kind of job they would most prefer in life, they will invariably reply that they want to work as members of a team. As so often with children they are of course absolutely right, because that is in fact how they will be working for the rest of their lives. We are, in many respects, trying to 'sell' them an inferior idea – the old-fashioned idea of the ladder. On the ladder you climb alone and as you climb it is in your interest that others should miss a rung and fall off; and just occasionally when nobody is looking you can even give them a shove to speed their descent.

> For in the end, on any reckoning, the ladder will never do; it is the product of a divided society, and will fall with it.(75)

The school therefore must be organized in order to put across to children the idea of *active mutual responsibility* and co-operation. And this has got to be done in the midst of an adult society which does not yet acknowledge this idea to anything like a great enough extent. In every school there will be variations in methods and approach depending upon the location of the school and the ability of the head. We want to see more, not less, scope for such variety. Our concern here is to draw attention to the essential framework of a school's organization without which it cannot possibly begin on the task.

Throughout his school career a child must have somebody to whom he can turn for help and advice, and sometimes criticism, on any conceivable topic which may arise. In a day school there are two ways of making sure that this is achieved. Either the child is the responsibility of his form-master or else he is the responsibility of his tutor. There are advantages and disadvantages in both systems. The form-master system is extremely effective during the first two years from eleven to thirteen, when children of the same age are taught in the same class for all subjects. An experienced form-master, who himself teaches his form of twelve-year-olds for at least one period every day of the week, very soon finds himself *in loco parentis* during the school day to these young children. Provided the children come from a good primary school and have reached the right standard of emotional and physical maturity, and provided they have all been equipped with the early linguistic and mathematical skills, the form-master at this stage can look after them very well. His greatest asset, if he is to win their (largely uncritical) confidence, is probably a sense of humour and loving care for their foibles and extravagances.

At the other end of the school, in the sixth form, the form-master comes into his own again. Here, on a basis of intellectual companionship experienced for the first time by children, it is the quality of his mind and his enthusiasm for his speciality which will make an impact. A really good sixth-form master probably has a greater effect than anybody – except parents – upon the life of an intelligent child. If the child has been lucky enough to meet such a person the effects may be lifelong. Years afterwards, when his own children need educating, it will be the presence of such a person at the school which will determine his wanting to send his own children there. From a practical point of view the sixth-form master provides the link between school and university for the children in his charge.

The main organization problem arises in the middle years between thirteen and sixteen. Forms begin to give way to setting after the first two years of a secondary-school course. (Setting is the grouping of children not according to their ages but according to their ability in one particular subject.) This is due to the importance which mathematics and science now assume in the curriculum. As the scope of mathematics widens and its pace increases, it is necessary to have mathematical sets that are carefully streamed according to mathematical ability. At the same time children must be setted either for general science or for separate classes in physics, chemistry, and biology. It seems quite probable that French, the main foreign language, would be more effectively taught in ability-sets, each leading to different papers in French at G.C.E. O-level. It is current practice however to leave the English subjects, English, history, and geography, as form subjects in which there is no setting for ability. Therefore the staffing problem is a difficult one. It is axiomatic that a form-master should take his own form at least once a day. Yet in the middle school the only man who can fulfil this requirement is the English teacher, for the historian and the geographer will probably not meet the form more than three times a week.

To overcome the difficulty some schools have introduced the tutorial system. When he moves into his third year the child joins a tutorial group which is organized on a vertical age-basis rather than the horizontal age-basis of a form. Each member of staff will have not more than about twenty children in his tutorial group and he will remain their tutor for these three years. A period must then be set aside each week for the tutorial groups to meet. During this time the teacher will discuss the child's work and out-of-school activities, and answer any problems that may arise. He will also be responsible for the child's discipline, and it will be the tutor who keeps in touch with the child's parents.

The middle-school tutorial system has disadvantages. The arguments that a child seeks his social milieu amongst his contemporaries is a strong one. In a tutorial group he finds himself in an artificial community in which his only valuable relationship is that which he develops with his tutor. It is rather like the boarding 'house' of a public school with the housemaster but without the companionship of the other members of the house. At the same time there is the practical disadvantage that in a day school there is very little time for a tutorial group to meet. If the tutor can spare no more than five or ten minutes for each boy in a week or fortnight it seems unlikely that anything worthwhile can be achieved. For these reasons we are inclined to reject the middle-school tutorial system, although there are certainly a few schools where it has been made to work effectively.

We consider that the middle-school problem of looking after children can best be met by creating the form unit according to the setting of mathematics. Under this system a child would learn, *in his form*, mathematics, science, English, history, and geography as well as being in his form for religion and ethics, current affairs, and physical education. He would be in a different group only for language study. English, history, and geography do not require to be settled and there is no reason why they cannot be taught just as well to groups of children collected together on a basis of mathematical ability as on any other basis. At the moment most schools create their middle-school forms on the basis of linguistic ability. We suggest that middle-school forms should be created on the basis of mathematical ability. We clinch the argument by the fact that mathematical setting is also the most suitable basis for scientific setting; children in the same mathematical set will be in the same set for science. Therefore, if forms were created on the basis of mathematical ability, it would be possible to keep children together in the middle school as a group for all subjects except foreign languages.

In the middle school, therefore, the form-teacher remains guide, philosopher, and friend to the child. The essential requirement is that he should see his children almost every day. It is this daily contact which will give him time to win their confidence and get to know them as individual people. Form-teachers under this system may be recruited from teachers of all the main subjects, except languages. For all will be in contact with the children for not less than three or four periods each week. Organized on such a basis the well-tried unit of a form and a form-teacher, which worked well in the days when a teacher taught all the main subjects to one form, could be made to work again. This would be the best way of looking after children during the years in the middle school.

Every teacher has experienced at some time or another the feeling that, however energetic he may stir himself up to be for a particular period, it will be of little avail – the children are just bored. If the teacher is tired he may drive himself on, using all the tricks of the trade, and yet he may still finish up with a lethargic or a restless class. It may be one of those summer afternoons when the sun is streaming in through the windows and boys' minds are far away on a week-end fishing expedition or some devilish mechanical project for the after-school hours. Or it may be the winter when the girls are concentrating on Christmas shopping in the local high street. But he knows, if he is wise, that they have 'shut down', that he won't get through that day any more. And many a teacher must at this point have reflected on the unnatural relationship which the classroom forces upon children for a very large number of hours during the most impressionable years of their lives. Unnatural because they have to sit, which is after all an adult occupation; unnatural because they have to spend so much time writing, which again was once a task for adults only; and finally unnatural because they want to create worlds and they have to listen so much to explanations of what has already been created. For children are pre-eminently the great 'doers' of the world and classrooms deny them that activity.

School societies are so important that they cannot be left to chance; they cannot be purely a voluntary activity that takes place for the energetic few after school hours. To make it possible for every child in a secondary school to participate in an activity *of his own choice* in school-time, four things are needed: instructors, space, equipment – and time. The question of time is most easily solved. We assume in our time-table a thirty-five period week. These periods can be covered effectively and include in a five-day week a complete games afternoon and two periods of another afternoon for societies. Two periods of society time is enough, on a weekly basis, to get something worthwhile done, especially if one remembers that quite a number of children will probably stay on for longer once they get really interested in what they have chosen to do.

Societies which meet in school-time can of course be under the care of a member of staff. In a good school there are very few members of staff now who do not undertake some out-of-school activity. This tradition that a teacher's work in England does not stop when he leaves the classroom is one of the most valuable things about our education. By extending this idea we are building upon this tradition. It may be that the society, usually referred to as a club, over which he presides is a specialist one in which the school provides an external teacher, say modelling or painting; in which case he may assume the role of administrator, encourager, and even student himself. Or it may be a club in which he instructs himself, making use of a hobby of his own – perhaps photography or boat-building –

and relying purely upon his own versatility. We shall argue later, in Chapter 10, that the Degree in Education should equip young teachers with enough skill to teach a hobby to children. But, in whatever capacity, it will be a condition of his appointment that he will be required to undertake the supervision of one of the school clubs. Inevitably the range of activities that any school can offer will depend not only upon the staff but also upon the buildings and equipment. But this is scarcely an insuperable problem once the club activities are regarded as an integral part of the school curriculum.

We hesitate to define in detail the scope of a school's club activities. But as they will be in the timetable they will involve all children up to the end of their fifth year and probably during their first year in the sixth as well. Children will perhaps opt out only when a year's experience in the sixth form has changed their interests. For the emphasis in society activities will be on the 'doing' rather than the 'talking'. The sixth-former may prefer to concentrate on his advanced work and take part in the special sixth-form type of society for which by then he may have acquired an appetite – debating, for example. An essential feature of the societies, however, will be that the child will be able to choose which he wishes to attend and that as far as possible their policy and control shall be in the hands of their senior members. The teacher's part will consist of such instruction as may be necessary and general supervision. In each club the object will be to have tasks, plays, projects, exhibitions, and so on in which each child can take part and learn to create something alongside his fellows.

Why are clubs and societies an essential feature of the curriculum? Children are seldom, if ever, emotionally involved in ordinary classroom work. Good teaching can capture their interest and good technique on their part can bring them substantial examination rewards. By this process their minds are sharpened but their feelings are left unexplored. If man were a wholly rational creature such a mental training would be ideal. But of course man is not wholly rational and he takes all the really big decisions of life on instinctive rather than on rational grounds. In club activities of his choice a child will be emotionally involved. He will be creating rather than hearing how other people have created. He will be cooperating as a member of a team rather than competing as an isolated individual. He will be working with his senses trained upon the material world rather than brooding with his mind upon literary forms. John Dewey has pointed out that we have neglected the training of the emotions in modern education:

> What do teachers imagine is happening to thought and emotion when the latter gets no outlet in the things of immediate activity? Were they merely kept in temporary abeyance, or even only calloused, it would not be a matter of so much moment. But they are not abolished; they are not suspended; they are not suppressed – save with reference to the task in question. They follow their own chaotic and undisciplined course. What is native, spontaneous, and vital in mental reaction goes unused and untested, and the habits formed are such that these qualities become less and less available for public and avowed ends.(12)

Clubs and societies are one of the ways in which we can seek to direct these qualities in the right direction.

A games afternoon forms another essential feature of the school week. We have already discussed the organization of physical education (see page 92 ff.) in which school games play an important part. Compulsory games are essential for the majority of children, up to the sixth form at any rate, and there are strong arguments for making children take part in team rather than individual events. Now that children are no longer sufferers from malnutrition with all its consequences for the development of physique and bodily coordination, games-playing affords much greater pleasure than it could ever do in the past. There is no reason why most children should not leave school able to play two or three games to a standard that will give them real relaxation and the chance of maintaining physical fitness after they leave school.

Our aim is to teach children at school the idea of *active mutual responsibility*. We want to encourage them in every possible way to develop their own powers of judgement and discrimination. This will involve giving far more thought to the community life of most schools than has yet been envisaged. It will involve the difficult but not impossible task of never setting children tasks and duties for which they cannot see at any rate a partially rational explanation. It will involve persuading them that they cannot have it both ways; if school is to be made less irksome they must become more responsible.

> You can't talk to people like that today. You're a man at fourteen; why don't parents and schools see that and treat us properly as grown-ups?[(73)]

Of course they're not grown-ups, but if we want them to become responsible grown-ups we must discover their potential and do everything in our power to help them develop it. The techniques they learn at school will soon be superseded, but the attitudes, positive or negative, which they develop will be a permanent possession.

Children's attitudes are formed to a great extent by the discipline of the school. If the discipline is too harsh, as it was very often under the earlier versions of the prefectorial system, order will be achieved at the expense of a conformist attitude on the part of the majority and a blind superiority on the part of the minority; the sort of nineteenth-century superiority in the pattern of prefect and fag, which in this century 'is going to cause revolutions, not profit from them'.[(40)]

How might they learn to govern themselves? The crux of the matter is to enlist the interest and enthusiasm for self-government amongst the older boys and girls and to enlist it on the widest possible basis. This is something perhaps which American schools have developed more effectively than English schools. It is not easy to graduate from an American high school without having been involved in some post of responsibility in the administration of the school community. It is something which the really good boarding schools teach their children. It is something which the best youth clubs have, or the best school football teams, or the best units in the Army Cadet

Force, or the best Scout troops, or the best work camps. It is the modern version of 'morale' which must be based today on *active mutual responsibility.*

The fallacy of the prefectorial system in today's conditions is that it is too narrow a basis on which to run a school community. What frequently happens is that a small group of children, the prefects, become isolated from the rest of the school and their authority and example thus lose their effect. It is really a system that suited the nineteenth century, when an extremely small group of men and women controlled the administration of this country and the colonial empire. Not infrequently it was that same small group that had formed the prefectorial groups of the public schools. Modern conditions have thrown all this overboard and today, and as far as we can see in the future, more and more responsibility will be attached to being a member of a team, to working together and contributing ideas and beliefs to the work of the team. The crying need today is for leaders who will lead from the shop floor rather than the office desk.

Instead of the prefectorial system we should like to see a School Society which would be the self-governing organ of the community. Each school club would send one of its members, presumably its secretary, to this Society. All the Captains of school games would be members. And each sixth form would be represented. The Society would elect annually its own executive committee. This committee would be presided over by its chairman – the phrase 'head boy' or 'head girl' is quite anachronistic nowadays. The Society would meet weekly, usually under the presidency of the head or deputy head. The executive committee and chairman would in fact be chosen in consultation with the head (and members of the staff) who would have the power of veto on any elections.

What kind of authority should the School Society have? Its membership will be composed of children representative of all the many interests in the community life of the school. The youngest child will feel that his interests are looked after by the secretary of his club. Because he himself has made a free choice of his club he will feel that he has also freely chosen a member of the self-governing body. The same sense of free choice will govern the attitudes of others towards their representatives. In practice of course the School Society will be composed mostly of sixth-formers as the clubs will contain children of all ages and the secretaries will obviously be elected from the older members. From his first days in the school, however, a child will feel a link with the authority that governs him. He will begin to learn the meaning of *active mutual responsibility*.

It will be the School Society which will be responsible for the routine day-to-day administration that now falls to the hands of prefects in many schools. Disciplinary offences will be offences against a self-elected body and therefore offences against the community as a whole. Therefore the task of punishment should be undertaken by the community and not by individual persons. Disciplinary offences will best be noted by members of the School Society in the course of their duty and the appropriate corrective action taken by the teaching staff. We want the School Society to lead by example rather than by sanctions.

The advantage which the School Society will have over the prefectorial system will be that it will teach children to co-operate for positive rather than negative ends. The prefectorial system is anachronistic because it largely limits children 'to the regulation of undesirable activities among themselves',(51) and does not set out to teach them how to work together for the common good. Because of this it bears no relation to life outside the school where men and women are involved in a network of communal enterprises. Bearing in mind the fact that in most schools prefects are appointed by the head with no reference to the wishes of other older children, the prefectorial system is as near a reproduction of authoritarian rule as can be conceived in a Lilliputian world. Under such a system it is no wonder that the majority of children, who have felt during their school lives no sense of mutual responsibility, should leave school with extremely rudimentary ideas about how to get along with their fellow men.

Of course self-government in schools is necessarily self-government within a limited sphere and subject at every stage to the veto of teachers. But there are a variety of ways in which the School Society can exercise its own autonomy. The running of clubs and games are the first obvious example. The planning and presentation of exhibitions provide another field of activity. So often exhibitions are misconceived because they are regarded as no more than a display of showpieces executed by the more talented children on the orders of the teacher. The object should rather be to exhibit on lines which the children have themselves conceived under the guidance of a teacher. In a school exhibition the important thing is the degree of participation by individual children and not the achievement of perfection by the teacher. Dramatic activity is another field. Dramatic standards in a school are usually set by an annual school play which is directed by a teacher and which aims consciously at perfection within the limitations of children's acting. But there is also a great deal of scope for the production of drama at lower levels, when the entire enterprise is under the control of the older children only advised by one of the teachers. Another task awaiting the school society will be the organization of the school dance, which may take place on the school premises once or twice a year. This can be most efficiently organized by the members of the School Society helped by a member of the staff who may undertake the role of compère.

The School Society must have within its competence the collection and expenditure of a certain amount of public money. This is very important, perhaps even vital, in training children about the relationship between money and society. We note in passing that the more far-reaching of the educational experiments in self-government have always stressed the importance of children controlling the money spent on their community activities. Fortunately the control of public money is probably less liable to abuse today than it may have been in the past when children had much less of everything than they have today. The three principles governing the School Society's money should be that the amounts involved should be limited and related to the possible objects of expenditure; that there should within these limits be free choice and therefore the possibility that mistakes will be made; and that the society should meet frequently to approve and criticize expenditure.

Sources of income for the School Society will be from various quarters. Clearly the whole idea, when introduced into a school for the first time, will be built up slowly from the bottom. We shall not present children, for instance, with the large sum of money needed to run a school game and ask them to allocate expenditure. On the other hand we can begin by diverting to the control of the Society part of the funds normally available for the sixth-form clubs and societies and asking them to debate the proportion of expenditure on these different activities. The clubs and societies about which we have spoken will be in endless need of comparatively small amounts of money for expansion and replacements and these needs will soon come under the control of the School Society. Early expenditure will also involve those small but essential amenities which older children expect to have in a good school: newspapers and magazines in the library, gramophone records, entertainment including lecture fees for a programme arranged each term by the Society itself, and at a later stage the control of the games fund itself.

So far we have gone with practical experience as our guide. Some will say that a school should go further and introduce a taxation system as well as a system of expenditure if the lessons are to be really learnt. We think that time alone in a day school prevents the running of such a system although it has been worked with great effect in boarding schools. Some will say that there is little point in having such an elaborate form of School Society. After all children will pick it all up after they leave school in any case. (So they will say.) Self-government is a long-term investment and we shall not see its results until today's children reach full maturity. But the governing boards of many of our public institutions today are an eloquent witness to the fact that democracy does not just go on existing – it either expands or withers up. If it is to expand in this country we must begin by expanding it in secondary schools.

The kind of school community that we have outlined already exists in our good schools. One can detect it by the amount of purposive activity that is going on in the school. Behind it all there stands the talent and enthusiasm of the teachers. Such a community can hardly fail to make a lifelong impression upon generations of children. Long after the daily details of their school lives have been forgotten the positive attitudes which they experienced will be retained. For a good education should build up in children the right sort of morale. The school which both challenges and cares for its children will succeed in doing this.

CHAPTER 10

The Teaching Profession

UPON the teaching profession depends the quality of our education. There are three problems which are essential background knowledge to any discussion of the recruitment and training of teachers. First the problem of quantity: there are 300,000 teachers and three out of every five are women. There are three women teachers in primary schools for every man teacher, and five men teachers in secondary schools for every four women teachers. Are there enough teachers to staff the schools? Secondly, the problem of quality: recognized teachers have qualifications which vary from two-year training to First-Class Honours or higher degrees plus a teaching diploma. Taking a broad division between graduates and non-graduates, we find that in grant-aided establishments in England and Wales 13·4 per cent of the women teachers and 32·1 per cent of the men teachers are graduates. Are the teachers in primary and secondary schools sufficiently well qualified for their job? Thirdly, the problem of teacher-pupil ratio: this is the ratio of the number of teachers on the staff to the number of children in the school and will only be the same as the size of the class if all the teachers are teaching at the same time exactly equal classes. Is the ratio low enough to enable the individual teacher to communicate in the most effective manner with the child? For teachers and children spend the major part of their time working in classrooms. This work cannot be really well done unless these three problems have been satisfactorily solved. The reason why the right conditions are essential for good teaching has been explained by Gilbert Highet:

Teaching is not like inducing a chemical reaction: it is much more like painting a picture or making a piece of music, or on a lower level like planting a garden or writing a friendly letter. You must throw your heart into it – you must realize that it cannot all be done by formulas, or you will spoil your work, and your pupils, and yourself.(24)

Table 3 outlines the facts.

Table 3 *The Quantity and Quality of Teachers*

QUANTITY

Percentage of 300,000 teachers in different types of schools

	MEN	WOMEN	MEN *and* WOMEN
Primary	14	41	55
Secondary	25	20	45
Total:	39	61	100

QUALITY

Percentage of teachers in different types of schools who are graduates

	MEN	WOMEN	MEN *and* WOMEN
Primary	7·8	2·6	3·9
Secondary Modern	20·2	13·7	17·3
Secondary Grammar	82·7	73·2	78·6
Secondary Independent	87·6	61·7	78·1

PUPIL: TEACHER RATIO

	LOCAL EDUCATION AUTHORITIES	INDEPENDENT
Primary	29·4	12·5
Secondary	21	12·1

Source: *Education in 1959*, the Report of the Ministry of Education and Statistics of Public Education in England and Wales (Command Papers), H.M.S.O., London, 1960.

What kind of men and women do we want in the teaching profession? There is a good deal of relevance in the old gibe that 'Those who can, do; those who can't, teach.' There is relevance because it reveals the fact that teaching, even today, is scarcely a profession. There are university lecturers whose discourses reveal that they know nothing whatever about teaching; there are educational administrators who act in a way that shows that they have never stopped to consider for one moment the obligations due to members of a profession; there are teachers whose actions sometimes indicate little of the sense of responsibility which is the mark of a professional person. And finally, there is the public which still in so many cases thinks that the teaching profession exists simply to keep Johnny off the streets between nine o'clock in the morning and four o'clock in the afternoon. Not yet, in fact, have we decided the kind of people we need as teachers and the kind of conditions we need to attract them.

What kind of people do we want? The two essential qualities are intellectual distinction and sympathetic understanding of young people. A teacher should have the sort of mind that retains a smack of radicalism through life. This will enable him to keep one foot firmly planted in the future where the test of his work will lie. At the same time he needs a great measure of human understanding and sense of responsibility which will enable him to play his part in forming the character of young people. To both these tasks he must bring confidence and enthusiasm in greater measure than the powers of criticism which he must also employ. For one of his jobs is to help adolescents to believe in themselves. There are other very important but not essential qualities. Teachers are lucky if they also happen to be all-rounders, versatile both in mind and hand, ready to meet the young on ground of the young's own choosing and so to canalize young enthusiasm down ways that have already been approved. They are also lucky if they have administrative gifts because young people are attracted by the well-organized enterprise, not yet being accustomed to the standard inefficiencies of adult existence. They have another advantage if they are clearly people who live in the macrocosm of the outer world as well as in the microcosm of the school world. For adolescents can be greatly influenced when they feel that they are being taught by mature men and women who are prepared to regard them as young adults rather than overgrown children. Composed of men and women with these qualities, backed up by efficient, businesslike administration, and led by a head with a talent for getting the best out of his team, a school should be able to carry out its task. The results, of course, lie far in the future.

What are the conditions necessary to attract such people and to keep them in teaching? We have already shown that a wide range of quality is required in the teaching profession and we feel that new entrants to the teaching profession may very well compare the career structure offered to them with that in other professions. No comparison would be entirely just and we have selected the average salaries earned by an administrative civil servant, a general medical practitioner, and an executive civil servant. These professions demand the same entrance requirements from the school-leaver as does the teaching profession, and they offer a salary-scale that is not high by comparison with actuaries, graduates in industry, dentists, solictors, or officers in the armed forces. In the first place, would-be entrants into each of the three professions requirc similar qualifications. The future administrative civil servant, general practitioner, executive civil servant, and teacher all require an academic qualification on leaving school ranging from five passes at G.C.E. O-level to two or three passes at G.C.E. A-level. The A-level passes are required to gain university entrance and entrance to the better teacher-training colleges: the O-level passes are necessary for entrance to the rest of the teacher-training colleges and to the medical school of a hospital. Of course each of these three professions will also obtain a number of more highly qualified people, but the important point is that the minimum qualifications are the same. These are the salary scales which will be one of the factors weighing upon a sixth-form child at school when he is choosing his career.

Secondly, there are the obvious differences in the maximum salaries paid at the top of each scale and also the differences in the rate of growth.* Both the administrative civil servant and the general practitioner, when they are on their maximum, receive at least £1,000 more than the teacher. Should the teacher

* For reasons of clarity we have discussed salaries in the concrete terms of those current in January 1961. Inevitably the reader will find the actual figures out of date as the over-all level of salaries rises, but we hope that in this way our proposals can be seen in their correct perspective.

have become head of a department, or even deputy or head of a school, he will still receive at least £500 less than the other two. And the executive civil servant, who is in most cases not as well qualified as the teacher, also receives on his maximum £500 more than the teacher. A comparison of rates of growth is more striking still. Although the general practitioner forfeits two to three years of salary on his training, by the age of thirty he is already earning over £500 more than the teacher. The administrative civil servant may be better qualified than the majority of teachers, but his qualifications are scarcely worth an extra £750 at the age of thirty. The executive civil servant starting at a lower salary tops the teacher's salary at the age of thirty-five.

There is therefore a serious discrepancy between the qualifications required at the point of entry into the teaching profession and the salaries paid to experienced teachers during their professional career. The would-be civil servant or doctor knows that by the age of thirty he will be rewarded for the sacrifices he has made in order to become a professional man: the teacher can be fairly certain that he will not be rewarded. Diagram 6 illustrates the average salaries offered to would-be entrants to the administrative Civil Service, the medical profession, the executive Civil Service, and the teaching profession.

A glance at the principles underlying the teacher's salary compared with those of the other professions, and indeed compared with the salaries paid in the industrial world, will reveal the cause of such discrepancy. The salary of teachers is a *single* scale which proceeds upwards by annual and equal increments (except the final one) until at the age of thirty-seven to forty the maximum is reached. The teacher starts with a salary that is in no way inferior to that in the other professions. His rate of growth consists of annual increments of £27 10s. with a final increment of £40. On his maximum he finds himself in a greatly inferior position to other professions and to industry. For they have adopted not one but a series of salary scales. On rising from one salary scale to the next the civil servant or the businessman receives a jump in salary which may outdistance

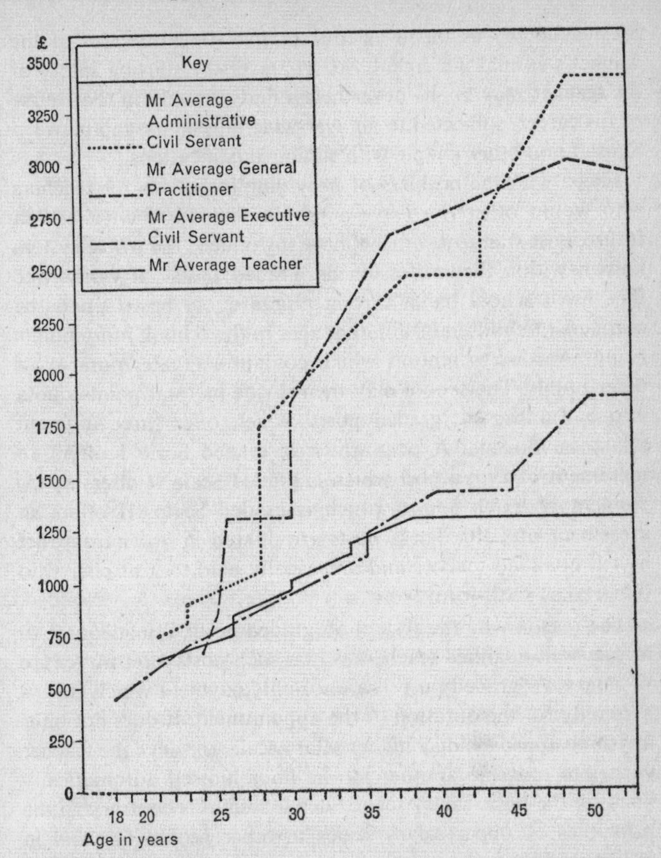

Diagram 6 *A Comparison of Average Salaries, January 1961.* 'Mr Average' is a median value used here to illustrate the 'career structure' as well as average earnings. The increments have been smoothed, but changes from one scale to another are represented by vertical lines. Sources: GP – Royal Commission on Doctors' and Dentists' Remuneration 1957–60, Cmd 939; ACS & ECS – Data supplied by Civil Service Commission; T – Report of Burnham Committee 1959 (allowance £210 and Pass Degree).

the teacher by as much as four or five times the size of the teacher's annual increment. So, whatever the starting salary of the teacher may be, he nevertheless finds himself, in the course of his career, subjected to an ever-widening salary gap between himself and other people with similar qualifications.

Faced with the problem of providing incentives for teachers who would otherwise leave a profession with such a barren future, post-war governments have introduced the whole system known within the profession as 'graded posts'. It works like this. Each school has a certain points quota based upon the numbers of children of different ages in the school, more points being awarded to schools which contain a greater number of older pupils. The school may then divide its total points quota into a number of 'graded posts' which offer three different salary increments. A post which is graded Scale I offers an increment of £90; a post which is graded Scale II offers an increment of £150; a post which is graded Scale III offers an increment of £210. These posts are offered in order to attract a well-qualified teacher and are usually paid to a teacher who undertakes sixth-form work.

The reason why the system of 'graded posts' is inadequate to attract well-qualified teachers is that such posts offer no tenure of salary. A 'graded post' is a once-only payment which is payable only for the duration of the appointment. It does not offer anything approaching a higher salary scale, for once the teacher wishes to move to another job he finds himself automatically back on the basic salary scale. Such a system is contrary to the principles of upper salary scales in other professions and in industry, where a man who is employed on an upper salary scale has complete security of salary, subject only to the termination of his job because of professional incompetence. In other words other professional men can move freely within the different sections of their profession without suffering a drop in salary whenever they move; the teacher cannot.

It is not so very long since a government spokesman, replying to a question about the salary offered to the new Chairman of British Railways, replied that in order to get the right man for the job it was necessary to offer a salary at competitive market rates. The present teachers' salary scale does not offer this type of salary. Clearly the teacher's salary does not compete with the other professions with which we have compared it; certainly it is not competitive with the salaries that are paid in industry. Unless a competitive salary scale is offered to would-be entrants to the teaching profession there is no prospect of Britain's having the kind of education she deserves.

In Chapter 1 we drew attention to the grave shortage of mathematicians and scientists in the teaching profession. Why should we not pay mathematicians and scientists a higher salary than those who teach the humanities? Mathematics and science are more marketable qualities *today* than English, history, or French. Without a very much higher standard of mathematical and scientific teaching as well as many more teachers of these two subjects in the schools, the whole structure of higher technological education will collapse. Why not solve the problem by offering the mathematicians and scientists more money?

Fortunately this solution has so far been resisted, despite the reiteration over the last few years (almost day by day) of the shortage of mathematicians and scientists. For we are planning for *tomorrow* as well as for *today*. Now we already know that *tomorrow* we shall need many more technologists. We are also beginning to grasp the fact that we shall need a much higher standard of general education amongst these same technologists, and indeed amongst everybody else. For example, we shall need a great deal more knowledge and judgement in the field of industrial relations. We shall need a more informed and a more critical electorate. We shall need a constantly alert public opinion *vis-à-vis* the control and the quality of mass communications. We shall need many more people who are concerned with the place of the creative arts in our society. The teachers of *today's* humanities and their successors will be the people concerned with *tomorrow's* general education. Later in this chapter we shall argue that the teaching profession will benefit immensely from having people who have received a sufficiently broad training to be able to keep a foot in both camps: specialist mathematicians with a good appreciation of the value of the humanities; specialist arts teachers who understand enough science to be able to appreciate the impact of science on society. All we do now is to point out that a salary scale which would have the effect of creating a better-paid group of mathematicians and scientists working alongside a lower-paid group of linguists, historians, and geographers would be a disaster.

There is therefore no alternative but to offer a competitive salary to the teaching profession as a whole. Such a competitive salary we shall call the *H–Y* salary scheme. The aim of the *H–Y* salary scheme will be to provide a career structure for teachers that can be compared financially with the other professions open to similarly qualified school-leavers. The object of the *H–Y* salary scheme will be to raise the over-all financial position of Mr Average Teacher to the point where he will feel, for the first time in our society, that he is adequately rewarded for a responsible job. The basis of the *H–Y* salary scheme is the provision of two salary scales which are closely correlated to the capacity of the teacher and the quality of his work.

On Scale A there is a twenty-five-per-cent rise on the 1959 Burnham scales. The annual increments are increased from £27 10s. to £30 and are extended to run over twenty instead of seventeen years. This produces a Basic Scale A for the three-year-trained teacher which starts at £650 and rises to £1,250 after twenty years' teaching. On top of this basic scale there are three flat increments for qualifications obtained:

1. An increment of £100 for a University Degree or for a Degree in Education;*
2. An increment of £200 for a University Degree and a Diploma in Education;
3. The addition of three annual increments for a First-Class Honours Degree, and the addition of two annual increments for a Second-Class Honours Degree. The maximum salary that can be gained on Scale A will therefore be £1,450 after seventeen to twenty years' teaching.

* See page 207 for a full discussion of the Degree in Education.

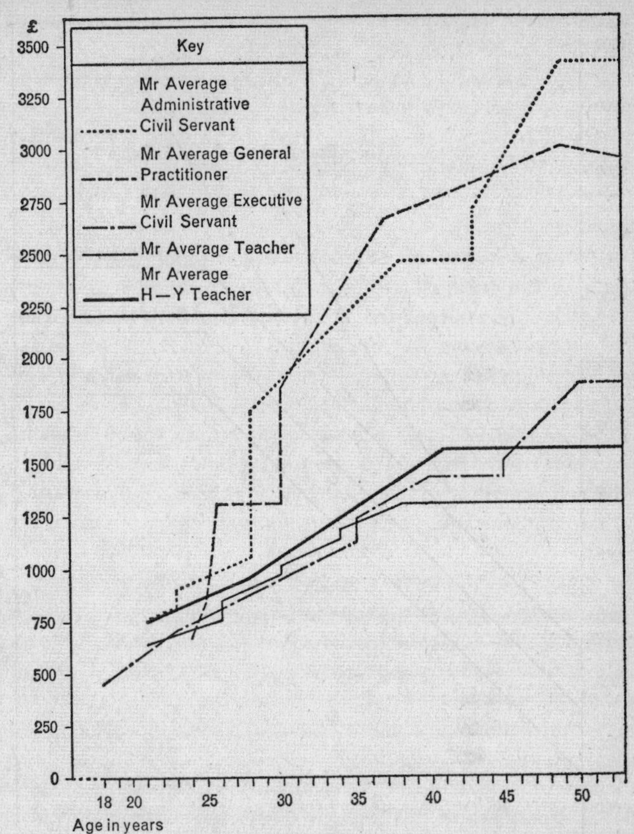

Diagram 7 *A Comparison of Average Salaries with the* H–Y *Scheme.* 'Mr Average' is a median value used here to illustrate the 'career structure' as well as average earnings. The increments have been smoothed, but changes from one scale to another are represented by vertical lines. Sources: GP – Royal Commission on Doctors' and Dentists' Remuneration 1957–60, Cmd 939; ACS & ECS – Data supplied by Civil Service Commission; T – Report of Burnham Committee 1959 (allowance £210 and Pass Degree). Mr *H–Y* Average Teacher has a Pass Degree with £262½ (£210 plus 25 per cent), i.e., approximately an arithmetic mean of Scale A and Scale B.

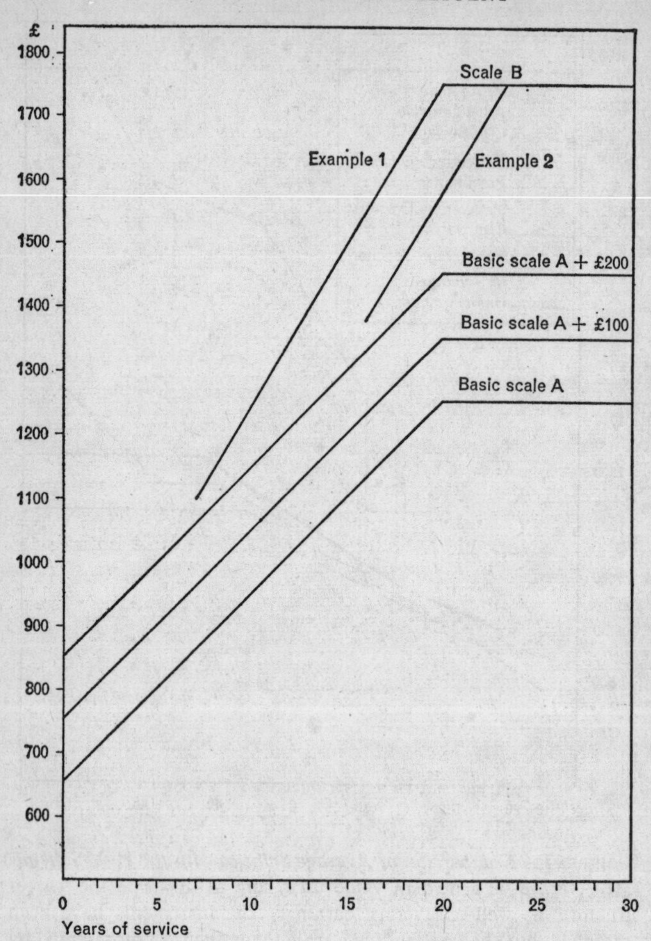

Diagram 8 *The* H–Y *Salary Scale*. Maximum on Scales A and B can be reached only after a minimum of twenty years except by advancement for First- or Second-Class Honours Degree.

Example 1: Promotion to Scale B after seven years' service with increments of £50 p.a.

Example 2: Promotion to Scale B after sixteen years' service with increments of £50 p.a.

Scale B does not commence until a teacher has completed seven years' service (four years in the case of First-Class Honours, etc.). Scale B provides an initial increase of £250 above Basic Scale A and it rises by annual increments of £50 to a maximum of £1,760 which can again be reached after a minimum of seventeen years' teaching. At any point in a teacher's career it would be possible to move from Scale A to Scale B, but of course the later he moves the longer it will take him to reach his maximum. With the introduction of the two scales, allowances would remain for head teachers, deputy head teachers, and heads of departments. Allowances for graded posts would be abolished.

Diagram 7 illustrates the position of Mr *H–Y* Average Teacher in comparison with the other professions we have already mentioned. Diagram 8 illustrates the *H–Y* salary scheme itself: on Basic Scale A the three levels of salary represent the increments for qualifications obtained; on Scale B there are examples of teachers who reach the scale both early and later on in their teaching careers.

How does a teacher make the advantageous move from Scale A to Scale B? Scale B posts, which would be advertised as senior posts, would be allocated to schools on a quota basis based on the size and the type of school, calculated on something like the present system of points quotas to which we have already referred. Once the new salary scales have been in operation for some years we consider that the greater numbers of qualified teachers applying for these posts may make it possible for local education authorities to increase the number of senior posts in their authority in order to improve the quality of their education. This would have the effect of enabling an authority to raise educational standards by bidding for better teachers. But this should not be introduced until the supply of well-qualified teachers is sufficient to fill adequately the minimum number of senior posts on a nation-wide basis.

Senior posts will form part of a career-structure attractive to a new entrant to the profession. They will offer an opportunity to the gifted but less well qualified teacher to be promoted on the merit of his work. And they will leave the gateway of promotion open to teachers in all types of schools.

Senior posts will also offer an incentive for a wide range of teachers. In the first place it seems probable that they will be awarded mostly to holders of a degree. The Degree in Education will enable many more college-trained teachers to compete for these posts on an equal footing with teachers who have been trained at a university. Secondly these posts will give greater flexibility to heads, who will be able to use them to appoint well-qualified and experienced men from another school as well as to promote able and loyal colleagues from among their own staffs. Thirdly, it should enable schools in the less attractive parts of the country to offer greater incentives to teachers to make a long-term move to their school. And lastly there is the very important fact that the existence of Scale B will act as a powerful stimulus to teachers to improve on their initial qualifications by taking the Degree in Education.

The advantages of Scale B over the present system of graded posts are numerous. Once he has reached Scale B a man will have security of tenure on that scale. There is therefore little chance that a good teacher will be forced out of the profession by purely financial reasons when he finds family responsibilities bearing heavily upon him in his thirties and forties. Scale B offers an adequate reward to the man who would prefer to teach his subject rather than become a head or even a departmental head. We consider it offers enough financial incentive to the mathematician and scientist who would really like to teach but under present circumstances turns somewhat reluctantly to industrial research. Most important of all Scale B, although not a rich man's salary scale, compares with the salary scales of other professions and of industry.

Scale B would, we think, have one further important educational bearing. The tendency in schools today is towards increasing size and a greater range of activities. To some extent this development has invalidated the old and hierarchical structure of responsibility vested in the head and through him in the deputy head and a few departmental heads. More and more we require a greater number of experienced and able men to handle administrative responsibilities formerly performed by the head himself. The handling of careers and the placing of children in suitable jobs has become a complicated and most important part of a teacher's responsibility. If schools are to adopt a form of 'in-training' for young teachers (see page 208) the supervision of such training will also require a great deal of care and wisdom on the part of the experienced teacher. And the expansion of sixth forms will require a similar type of man. Scale B would surely make more of these men available. As with the immensely responsible position of the housemaster in a public school, you would be paying a good salary to a man and asking him at the same time to undertake a more responsible position.

The *H–Y* salary proposals would be costly. A recent memorandum,[4] based on the salaries which were paid to teachers before the 1959 Burnham award, estimated the cost of similar proposals 'in the region of £70 m.'. The *H–Y* scheme could not in our opinion be achieved satisfactorily without a greater proportion of the national income being spent on education. We consider, however, that it would do more than any other factor to establish a first-rate teaching profession. Scale A would provide for the first time an adequate reward for the average teacher as well as for the non-career teacher who may leave teaching for marriage after a number of years. Scale B would provide sufficient incentive to attract into teaching a fair share of the brains and ability in the country; having attracted them it would pay them enough to prevent their leaving for financial reasons and at the same time it would thrust into their hands a greater measure of responsibility. The adoption of the *H–Y* scheme would mean the end of state education on the cheap, but we think the proposals might receive the blessing of Sir Alexander Fleck, lately Chairman of I.C.I., who has long been a critic of English education:

> All this will cost money, perhaps more than has already been estimated. But many years in industry have convinced me that if you want something you usually have to pay for it.[40]

A radical change in teachers' salary scales will necessitate new negotiating machinery. When the Burnham Committee, which decides teachers' salary scales now, was founded in 1919 by H. A. L. Fisher, then President of the Board of Education, the intention was to increase the power of the local education authorities and to deny power to Whitehall. On the Committee there is an equal representation of local authorities and of teachers' organizations. The constitution of the Committee assumed that the education bill would continue to be met out of the rates rather than out of taxation. Now it is clear that the changes we propose in teachers' salaries are too costly to be placed on the ratepayer. In fact the Burnham Committee's composition precludes it from even contemplating such changes. It is fair to say that in 1919 'secondary education for all' was scarcely a serious possibility in this country. Now all that has changed and the time has come to place the responsibility for teachers' salaries, like those of the Civil Service, upon the government. Sir Percival Sharp, in his letter of resignation after thirty years' service on the Burnham Committee, said:

> I will not be a party to a procedure that shifts from the Minister of Education and the Chancellor of the Exchequer to our shoulders an arduous responsibility of denying justice to teachers.(68)

The time has now come to set up a Royal Commission on teachers' salaries empowered to consider not only new salary scales but also the method of payment.

In a war military problems are given high priority; in an epidemic medical problems are given high priority; when there is a wave of crime the police receive high priority: at all other times education should receive high priority. There is one very good reason why. Our children are our major investment in the future; we have relatively few years when we can look to the quality of our great investment; if the opportunity is lost, it will not recur. Every time the forward progress of education is delayed we run the risk of facing the future with inadequate resources. Sometimes we have to make up with greater expense for inadequate investment. For instance it costs seven times as much to keep a child in a reform school as to keep the same child in a secondary school. A sense of urgency should never be absent from discussion of educational reform.

But a look at the educational statute book is not reassuring. Take, for instance, the problem of further education for the fifteen to eighteen age-group in an industrial society. No less than sixty years ago Sir Michael Sadler campaigned for the provision of day continuation schools in this country. The Education Bill of 1918 made statutory provision for such colleges and nothing whatever happened. The Education Act of 1944 made statutory provision for county colleges and this remains one of the two major unfulfilled provisions of the Act. Finally, in 1959, they were again recommended by the Crowther Committee and interred by the House of Commons in 1960. Sixty years and two major Education Acts have made not the slightest difference.

There are over half a million people engaged in the field of education, of whom nearly 300,000 teach in the state schools. The rest either teach in the private schools (about 30,000) or are in educational administration; a large number are concerned with school meals and school health. In matters of educational reform such a large group should surely form a powerful stimulus to governmental and public opinion, as powerful, for example, as the British Medical Association. But professional educational opinion does not rank on a par with that of other professional bodies. This is because there is as yet no professional unity within the teachers' organizations which is empowered to express this opinion on the issues of major importance. The National Union of Teachers – the largest of these organizations – has recently put forward proposals for a single professional association. Such an association would be a federal body which would leave considerable powers to the individual member bodies. We argue strongly that there would be great advantages in such a body, as it would go a long way towards the raising of the public and governmental concern with the urgent educational problems of the country.

Pedagogy is a word much honoured by the Germans and much derided by the British. The legend that we are a nation of amateurs prevailed until very recently with regard to teachers. After all, did we not invent and teach the rest of the world so much of modern sport? Professional training was not necessary for sporting success. What more was teaching than a termly sporting event governed by a notion devoted to what the French call *le fairplay*? Our national literature is full of good-natured satire on the teaching profession; films and television have for long made play with the ridicule of schools and what goes on inside them. Until modern times teachers have borne the brunt of the deep-rooted anti-clerical tradition in Britain, often expressed with the utmost bitterness by the upper classes, who have had most to lose from the emergence of a well-educated nation. For these reasons the training of teachers has become a subject of national concern only in our own day. Until the McNair Committee of 1944 set up the first University Institutes of Education there was no nationally approved method of training teachers, and the study of teaching methods and principles in Britain was far in arrears of other countries, notably Germany and the United States.

The only way to provide adequate professional training for teachers is to institute for them a Degree in Education. Without such a degree we do not think there is any chance of having a united and well-qualified profession. Without such professional recognition the present division within the profession between graduate and non-graduate teachers will persist and probably widen. At the same time we shall find that the status of training colleges will fall *vis-à-vis* the status of universities. And we shall find the emergence more and more of two separate educational hierarchies clearly labelled 'first-class' and 'second-class'. For at the present time there is a grave discrepancy: the gulf which divides the three-year-trained graduate from the three-year-trained teacher. In the first instance it may have been largely a matter of luck that decided that one boy or girl gained a university place from school, whereas another gained a place in a teacher-training college. But at the end of three years of further education the university student is the holder of a degree, after which he can quite easily take a further year's training to become a qualified teacher. However, the training-college student, who has also had three years of further education, merely holds a certificate to say that he is a trained teacher – and he has made no progress towards becoming a graduate. When one remembers that there are large numbers of men and women in training colleges simply because Britain has a totally inadequate number of university places – to say nothing of the numbers who have been turned away from training colleges themselves for lack of places – it becomes clear that the training-college course should lead towards the same qualification as the university course. That it has not yet done so is due more than anything else to the old-fashioned snobbery of some universities.

The Degree in Education will be obtainable in four to five years after the student enters the training college. It will be designed in two parts and Part 1 will be taken after completing the training-college course. Part 1 will clearly be the theoretical part of the degree *par excellence*, although it will by no means exclude a certain amount of practical teaching experience. But on the completion of Part 1 the student will become the teacher and clearly he will no longer have the same amount of time for theory. In view of the fact that the period of training is the same as the period of training for a Pass or General Degree at the university, it would appear that the standard of Part 1 academically need not be very much inferior to the standard of the Pass Degree. In fact there is no reason why a student teacher who has completed Part 1 of a Degree in Education should not go on to take a Pass Degree externally as an alternative to the Degree in Education. On the salary scales which we propose (see *H–Y* scheme above) the Degree in Education and the university Pass Degree are to be equally rewarded. Scale B will provide a sound financial incentive to a young teacher to get his degree, whether at the level of a Pass or as a Degree in Education, in order to stand a better chance of promotion to the higher scale. The vitally important point about the Degree in Education will be that the three-year training-college student will have been enabled to get half-way towards graduate status.

The content of the Degree in Education will be best decided by a committee of men and women drawn from the faculties of the universities, the institutes of education, and the training colleges, and from the ranks of seasoned and successful teachers. If these three great areas of the educational world are fully represented a degree which is both academically challenging and pedagogically realistic should emerge. Its content will lie somewhere between the present university degree and the present diploma in education and will, we hope, include the best from each of these two courses of training. If the Degree in Education is to have any single feature which expresses the purpose of the whole it will surely be to re-establish the unity of education against the present sad, subject-ridden curriculum that goes by the name of secondary education. To do this will require the work of the best minds that the country can produce. It seems highly unlikely that many non-graduates will pass the bar from Salary Scale A to Salary Scale B and therefore there will be a great incentive to obtain a Degree in Education.

Upon leaving the training college the student becomes the teacher and proceeds to take his place in the front line. During this time he will also be preparing to take Part 2 of the Degree in Education. The next two years will be regarded essentially as a period of 'in-training'. In order to avoid the remarkably common practice of burdening the young and inexperienced teacher with a heavy and unrewarding timetable the regulations for the Degree in Education will have to legislate as regards the maximum number of teaching hours per week that may be given to a teacher under 'in-training'. Perhaps two-thirds of the total teaching time would be realistic, giving a maximum timetable during 'in-training' of twenty-three out of thirty-five periods. During 'in-training' it must also be accepted that the teacher would be under supervision and it might be accepted that any teacher holding a Scale B post or above could be responsible for such supervision, and could be required by the head to undertake it. There is little doubt that such arrangements would go a very long way towards easing the difficult early years in a teacher's career when many young men and women need help and encouragement. It would have the corollary of placing upon the schools and the senior members of the profession a definite responsibility for the training of the younger members. This is in line with the training pattern of every other great professional body. Indeed it is extraordinary, as a headmaster remarked very recently, that 'we [the teaching profession] are the last great professional body not responsible for our training methods'.(22)

Traditionally, the older universities, with one or two honourable exceptions, have been little interested in the education of the nation. Such an interest would be akin to expecting Fortnum and Mason to take the lead in settting up low-priced supermarkets in Piccadilly. The older universities, with their essentially narrow Honours schools, are tailored to meet the demands of another society in which an élite, and only an élite, filled all the professional and administrative posts in the country. Today they continue in this role backed up by their disproportionate prestige and by the simple and quite disastrous fact that an entirely inadequate provision of university places means that they can select one from every ten or twelve applicants and wash their hands of the rest. We do not blame them for this. But we do blame them when they step down from their ivory towers in order to suggest that much larger numbers of graduates will be harmful for the nation. Witness the recent most interesting correspondence under the title of 'Mass Graduation' in *The Times* which began with a letter suggesting that a reasonable aim would be for this country to train as many graduates by 1970 as will be trained in France – half a million. Clearly we must look elsewhere for support for the Degree in Education.

We must look towards the new universities and those which are still only on the drawing-board. These universities are already engaged in planning degree courses which will offer something entirely novel in their content. It is in these universities, for example, that we may expect to see the development of effective degree courses in sociology, a subject long derided by Oxbridge. Many of these universities will no doubt experiment with the idea of a foundation year of general studies, as has been initiated at the University of North Staffordshire. From them will come, in any case, many of the future teachers. Situated as they will be in the provincial cities of England and Wales they will be ideal centres for administering the Degree in Education, especially when we remember that Part 2 of the degree will have to be taken by teachers already deeply involved in a teacher's daily work, with little time for travel. For example, these universities will be the ideal places in which to arrange courses of evening lectures on education for Part 2 candidates. In fact, it seems very likely that these new universities will provide the essential stimulus without which the standard of work of the training colleges can never be effectively raised.

This then should be the pattern for the professional training of teachers. Coupled with the new salary scales we consider that it should scotch once for all the idea that teaching is a 'dead-end' occupation undertaken only by saints or fools. It will firmly establish teaching as a profession staffed very largely by graduates who have been specifically trained for the job they are going to do. Within the ranks of the teachers it will provide a sense of purpose, quality, and unity, combined with the knowledge that they are doing a job of tremendous importance and respected by the community which they serve. We consider that such a pattern would prove to be an investment of far-reaching importance for the future of Britain.

Finally, a few remarks upon the use of the teachers whom we have recruited and trained.

A world-wide shortage of trained teachers exists at the same time that the demand for their services constantly increases. For example the Commonwealth, in almost every case in far worse shape than ourselves, cries out for the seconding of teachers from Britain. Recently the British government have rightly agreed to help more than they have been doing in the past. Britain has a tremendous part to play in the teaching of the English language to millions of Asians and Africans who need the use of our language urgently. We cannot stand by and tolerate a situation whereby this teaching is performed by Russian (or even Chinese) teachers. If we are to play our part, and on a scale much larger than we have yet envisaged, we must ensure that we make much more efficient use of our teachers than we have been doing up to now.

The existing system of sixth-form teaching in schools is one place where considerable economy could be effected. So long as a grim contest for a few places at the older universities remains the pattern dominating all sixth-form work in schools, so long will we continue to employ some of our ablest men and women on the comparatively sterile task of pressurizing a very small proportion of boys and girls through these entrance requirements. If, however, the Honours courses at all universities – and especially the Honours courses in the natural sciences – were lengthened,* then the schools' task would stop upon the attainment of the Advanced Level of the G.C.E. This is the natural point where the school should hand over to the university; it would be much more economical in teaching manpower if this were so. From the point of view of the highly qualified teacher, who may hold First- or Second-Class Honours in his subject, there is the prospect of many new openings ahead for him in the field of higher education. If he is the academic type rather than the school-teaching type his work will probably lie at a training college or an institute of education. Movement to higher education from a school should therefore be much easier than it is at the moment. If, on the other hand, he decides that he is really more interested in education than in his subject pure and simple he will probably decide to remain in school-work, teaching to the Advanced Level and taking an increasing share in the administration of the school.

Once the Degree in Education and the new salary scales are established, a school will be very sparing of the way in which it employs its 'research-type' scientist in, for instance, the Ordin-

* A four-year course seems the right answer. See Chapter 8.

ary Level G.C.E. type of work. It will be possible, as is already done in a few of the public schools, to have a high standard of work in the body of the school undertaken by men who hold the Degree in Education or the General Degree, while reserving sixth-form work for highly qualified men and also allowing some time for them to set up first-class experimental demonstrations to be seen by the sixth form as a whole. For there is no doubt that it is fear of humdrum routine teaching which causes some able scientists to keep away from teaching. In this, as in all other ways, we must use our teachers as efficiently as we can.

Above the teacher stands the benevolent dictator of British education – the head. With the exception of one or two heads of famous public schools and grammar schools, these potentates are shadowy figures in the public mind compared to some of the civil or military persons of the state. Within the educational world, however, they wield a great deal of power at all levels of education from eleven plus to eighteen plus. They are organized in three tight groups: the Headmasters' Conference, which is mostly composed of the Independent and Direct Grant Schools; the Incorporated Association of Headmasters, which is composed of the rest of the secondary boys' schools; and the Incorporated Association of Headmistresses for the secondary girls' schools. Under these three associations comes the absolute control of the secondary curriculum, subject only to the requirements of the examining boards and the universities; under them comes the appointment of all the secondary staff, subject only to the approval of the governing bodies of their schools; in their hands lies the responsibility for the moral, mental, and physical welfare of over three million children. It is indeed surprising that only a few years ago it was calculated that no more than ten per cent of all these people received a salary of more than £1,500. In fact, if, as many people believe, the quality of heads has declined since the war, this could easily be because it is a better paid and less onerous job to be an educational administrator.

Can we define the job of the head under modern conditions? The task which he is called upon to perform is enormous. In a medium-sized secondary school he may have nearly fifty teachers on his staff. If he is going to use to the full the talents of these people he must direct, encourage, and inspire them. In the same size of school he is ultimately responsible for the education and upbringing of six or seven hundred children. Even to see the parents of these children for half an hour once during the school year will involve him in an immense amount of work. At the same time he is responsible for the physical plant of the school, for its maintenance, its renewal and enlargement. Very often he is a public figure required to represent the school and what it stands for to the outside world. Last, and perhaps most vital of all, it is his planning and forethought upon which the school depends for its influence upon the children. And all these tasks he performs very often with less clerical assistance than the leaders of most other large-scale enterprises.

There is no doubt that his success will depend on his ability to decentralize his numerous tasks. For secondary education is increasing in complexity as it improves in quality and more especially as more children stay on into the sixth forms of schools. In the 1930s the sixth forms were small and the range of education was far narrower than it is today. In those far-off days a head could afford to be little more than a kind of super sixth-form teacher who made a speech once a year on Prize Day. In those days education was not 'news' and a head paid little attention to such things as public relations. The 'bulge' had not even been heard of. The war and 1944 and the shortage of scientists have changed all that.

Under the *H–Y* salary proposals the head will also be able to decentralize effectively. On his staff there will be a sufficient number of senior teachers, earning a Scale-B salary, and ready and willing to undertake administrative responsibility. These men will not only undertake the administration of departments such as the organization of the mathematical or modern languages departments, but will also have clearly defined responsibility in the school as a whole. For example, in expanding sixth forms it is necessary to have not one but two or three teachers in charge of giving children advice about their careers. These teachers will have the great responsibility of becoming informed about the openings in an ever-widening field of careers and of advising the head about where to place children. Under the scheme for in-service training of teachers during the two years when a young teacher is studying for Part 2 of his Degree in Education, a senior teacher will be needed for their guidance and encouragement. Naturally the responsibilities undertaken by senior teachers will vary with each school. But the essential point is that these men and women will be available to share the head's load.

Once the load has been shared the head will have gained time to think and decide policy. By deliberately freeing himself from routine, which can now be left in the hands of able and responsible senior teachers, the head will be able to bring the full weight of his experience and vision to the guiding of the school. He will have time to encourage his staff in their work and to make plans for them to seize every opportunity to take refresher courses and keep themselves up to date in their subjects. He will have time to consider the content of the education which the school is offering. In particular at the present time he will be able to consider the question of the kind of 'general education' which he regards as being suitable for his sixth forms. He will devote some of his time to a keen and critical interest in the numerous and extremely important activities of the school which go on outside the classroom. And, in conjunction with his governors, he will spend time in making plans for the future and the enlargement of the purpose and effectiveness of the school. In these and many other ways his vision will be the guiding factor in the life of the school.

The head's responsibilities to parents will remain very considerable in all but the largest schools. (In a comprehensive school of 2,000 children, for example, the head must delegate even this responsibility to housemasters and tutors.) Although the head's knowledge of many of the children must depend largely on the information which he receives from the teachers who have contact with the child, he nevertheless remains as the key person in the eyes of the parents. He will spend a good deal of time interviewing parents and discussing their children with them. On these occasions he will also be availing himself of the opportunity to explain to parents the aims and ideals of the school and how the school is trying to help their particular child. He will probably spend a morning every week in work of this kind.

The head is also the representative of the school in the outside world. He cannot avoid public relations. If he is head of a city school, his school and to some extent education as a whole will be judged by what he says on public occasions, whether it be his annual Prize Day speech reviewing the recent school year or the few remarks which he makes after lunching at the Chamber of Commerce. Somehow the head must contrive on these occasions to break out for a while from what Charles Lamb called 'the world of the little people', and present himself and his work as part of a great profession concerned with the care and nurture of the nation's future men and women. There is no more effective way by which the nation can be brought to a realization of the tremendous importance of education.

Because the head's job is so exacting we suggest that he be appointed on a contract basis with plenty of opportunity for renewal. It should be perfectly possible for a head who has held an appointment for some years to move to another field of education altogether, if he wants to, without losing salary. This would also provide a perfectly reasonable way of moving a head whose contract the school governors did not wish to renew. Salary scales should be such that an ex-head could perfectly easily move on to the inspectorate or training-college work. We also suggest that there is an excellent case for establishing groups to undertake work study for education as a whole. In these groups former heads would have much to contribute. The lack of such freedom of movement at the moment has one serious inhibiting factor on education: it means that heads, on the whole, often stay too long at one school with the result that they go stale on the job. This has the effect of bringing apathy upon that particular school. But more important than this is undoubtedly the fact that apathetic heads prevent the younger men and women with the fresh ideas which are always needed in education from getting to the top. All professions face the problem of retiring their top men when they have passed their prime.

Above all we need vision and not dreams from our teachers. Young people look forward and not backward, and they can be led effectively only by men of vision, not by dreamers. It is significant that the best independent schools not infrequently appoint really young men to their headships. What they are doing is to invest in a man's vision even though he has had little chance to demonstrate his administrative efficiency. Surely history shows more often than not that men grow in capacity in accordance with the increasing range of problems and opportunities presented to them. One man of ideas is worth a score of men who are merely efficient. One man who knows where he is going is worth many who are merely travelling along the road.

As Highet said, teaching is an affair of the heart. We have outlined comprehensive proposals for recruiting and training teachers. There is no issue between these proposals and those who argue that the teacher must be a man 'with a vocation'. These proposals will not make any teacher a rich man. Teaching will remain a vocation as it has always been. But these proposals will ensure that men and women with a vocation for teaching can look forward to a career of service in which they will take their place alongside the other great professions whose work is respected by the community which they serve.

CHAPTER 11

The Architecture of the School

THE environment of a school is of great importance. The Athenians sent their boys to the palaestra and later to the gymnasium because of the importance they attached to physical education. In these stadiums, which were usually built in the shape of a courtyard, the boys learnt to emulate the great athletes of the day. Situated in the midst of the city, the boys were taught that their first duty to society was to develop and maintain their physique, whether for the peacetime games or for war. In the great days of Athens there was no conscription. Public service was a sufficient incentive to add military training to the sports of the gymnasium. The environment of Athenian upbringing at its best was sufficient to instil into boys the idea of public service. On the other hand, during the centuries after the fall of Rome, both religious and feudal practice was to educate boys in the privacy of the castle or the monastery. Such privacy for the young produced an era which was notorious for its lack of public spirit and the aggrandizement of private interest over the needs and aspirations of society. In the industrial age in which we live many of our schools are inevitably sited in cities and we can realize once again the Athenian ideal of the school set in the midst of the community.

If an Englishman's home is his castle, we should like to be able to say that an English child's school is his market place. Unlike the primary school, which has its closest link with the child's home, the secondary school should have its closest link with the town in which the child lives. Fortunately, the isolated type of secondary school is rarely built today and town planning should always ensure that the school is not far from the hub of affairs. For our age differs from the last because it is a democratic age. The nineteenth-century public school, for instance, standing in many acres of grounds in pleasant country, was the epitome of the end of an aristocratic era in which secluded privacy was the lot of the ruling class. Now we need schools which stand in the midst of towns and in the midst of suburbs because that is where tomorrow's rulers will come from. We want secondary schools to be involved in the life of the community.

Two great advantages accrue to education from such siting of schools. In the first place there is much more chance that a child will move happily and without frustration from school life to working life. The variety of the urban scene stimulates older children in the same way that it stimulates adults. There is nothing to decry in the maturity of London or Manchester schoolchildren compared with their contemporaries from the more relaxed countryside. Children do remarkably well in every way under urban conditions despite the romantic critics of our cities who sometimes speak as though the industrial revolution had never happened. In any case, there are today vastly increased opportunities for children to 'get away from it all' in holiday time. The second advantage is that if a school is sited not far from the hub of affairs it can be seen by the public. And it is becoming increasingly important that the public, whether as parents, citizens, or tax- and ratepayers, should not only know that education exists but should also be aware that education can be seen to be carried on. We want to encourage informed public opinion about the education of our children, and this is one of the ways in which it can be done.

There is scope for a great deal of imaginative experiment in relating the school to the life of the community. The idea of the Cambridgeshire Village Colleges has been an inspiring concept of how the education of country children can be effectively linked with the cultural needs of the community as a whole. At Impington, for example, school and adult education take place quite happily in a group of buildings specifically designed for both purposes. There are a number of facilities already used both by schoolchildren and by adults which, on account of their cost, cannot very often be provided solely for schools. Swimming-baths, theatres, and museums are obvious examples. There are numerous practical difficulties to be faced in providing such facilities on a communal basis. However, if county colleges are to be more than a pipe-dream in this century, it would be wise policy to start planning for them now. During the course of such planning many useful lessons would be learnt about combining facilities for school and adult education.

The problem is for us architects to make architecture out of a school, not for teachers, as otherwise happens, to try to make a school out of architecture.(66)

The delegates to the 1960 Milan International School-Building Congress were apparently startled, even shocked, by this assertion by a British architect. In the immediate post-war years, and under the stimulus of the Education Act of 1944, there was a new spirit abroad in school architecture: the idea that both architects and educationists should combine in the planning of schools. The first need was to build primary schools and Hertfordshire County Council, who built nearly fifty schools between 1946 and 1952, led the way in such consultation. J. M. Richards comments:

The informal planning of the post-war English school aptly reflects the needs of the English public education system in its transitional state, following recent legislation. The architects clearly found it stimulating to work in cooperation with educationists who were as much in experimental mood as they were.(48)

To what extent can school architecture assist or detract from the aims and objects of a secondary school? Before the 1944 Act there were no specific regulations for the building of schools. Schools were subject merely to the legislation which covered buildings in general; the most recent legislation had been the Public Health Act of 1936. The 1944 Act changed all this. Not only did it classify the types of building required for different types of school but it also laid down in considerable detail the minimum requirements for almost every conceivable unit in the school. It regulated the amount of space per child, both in and outside the building; it specified minimum requirements for classrooms, laboratories, workshops, gymnasia, and administrative offices; it stipulated the amounts of light and air-change in classrooms; it even produced a standard design for building pram sheds. For the first time those who planned new schools had adequate guidance in their task.

The effect of the Act has been that new schools have been better equipped to discharge their primary task of teaching than ever before. It is perfectly true that local education authorities have not always been able to meet all the requirements of the Ministry of Education. Money has delayed until recently the equipment of scientific laboratories. The London County Council originally planned to introduce separate drama halls into their schools, but had to cut them out when a cost-limit was imposed in 1952. There has never been with most authorities enough space or money to provide house rooms for children in the larger schools. Other instances could doubtless be quoted of how early recommendations have not been adequately met, but by and large the improvement in classroom conditions has been quite remarkable. And at the same time steps have been taken to modernize and add to existing school premises. From the child's point of view a great deal has been done to improve the environment in which he is taught; from the teacher's angle working conditions are greatly improved.

We take issue, however, with much of the new school building on other grounds. In 1436 the Duke of Suffolk founded at Ewelme in Oxfordshire a triple group of buildings: a hospital, a church, and a grammar school. Standing on rising ground this group of buildings is one of the most picturesque in England. Like the enclosed buildings of Eton or Winchester or the colleges of Oxford and Cambridge, these buildings had a purpose behind their construction which entitles them to be classified as architecture. They were designed to promote the idea of a learning community. They took as their example the best-developed community building of the age, which was the medieval house, with its hall and rooms grouped round a quadrangle. It was the quadrangle which became the essential feature of all community building from then until modern times. Communal life is fostered in quadrangular buildings because of the simple fact that the inmates of these buildings meet each other many times a day as they go about their business. Here was an architectural solution to an educational problem.

Supremely functional as many of our new schools are, the question remains – what is the purpose behind them?

Children, we believe, need every encouragement to develop their personalities. If they feel that at every stage of their life at school they form a significant part of the school community their personalities are more likely to grow than if they get the impression that the school is a kind of conveyor belt along which they pass, assembling a cumulative body of knowledge until they emerge as the finished product. For a child each stage of education should be a *finished* product in itself. Each year in a child's school life should mark a degree of accomplishment and growth. One of our architectural correspondents considers that above all secondary-school architecture should stimulate the child to further efforts and discoveries. Once the child is bored by his environment education will have failed in its main purpose of building personality. This aim, rather than the aim of functional efficiency, should be the purpose of a secondary school.

Post-war secondary-school building, however, has subordinated this aim to functional efficiency. We have in all new schools, not only the large ones, huge blocks of buildings which are purely functional in their purpose. The layout plans for these schools reveal this quite clearly with their neat divisions into functions: (1) teaching, (2) assembly, (3) workshops, (4) gymnasium, (5) schoolkeeper's house. Each unit is usually the result of much technical care and represents a great step forward from the school building of the past. The regulations of the 1944 Act are scrupulously observed: none more so than the provision of large expanses of glass to meet the regulation that 'two per cent of the natural light outside should fall on the darkest part of the classroom'.[23] Like the Palace of Green

Porcelain discovered by Wells's Time Traveller, these blocks stand solitary and impersonal, a monument to the technical efficiency of our age. In them there is no doubt that many children will receive technical instruction of a higher quality than in the past. But there is no evidence of any purpose behind them to educate a community of young people.

Is there a master plan which might achieve the aim of educating a community of children by developing their personalities to the uttermost while teaching them the techniques which they will need in the modern world? It is perhaps significant that there is no reference at all to modern school building in Sir Bannister Fletcher's *History of Architecture*. It is also significant that despite the immense increase in the educational expenditure of every country in the world we have been unable to find one of the world's most famous architects who has designed a secondary school. Our ancestors, as we have already pointed out, devised an architectural solution for the needs of a learning community. Can we not do as much for our schools?

The design of a secondary school should be once again quadrangular. Everything of significance should take place within the quadrangle; only physical education need be left outside. In the middle of the quadrangle the plan will place the buildings which belong to the whole community. Down the sides of the quadrangle will go the buildings required by different sections of the community. These sectional buildings will be grouped together so that each section will form a smaller community of its own. On one side of the quadrangle will be the entrance and administrative offices. By elevating the hall in the middle of the quadrangle adequate space will be provided for free play and circulation.

Diagrams 9a and 9b show the plan for such a school. The heart of the school is the assembly hall with its stage at one end and its display room at the other. The display room, which will be used for exhibitions both privately within the school and publicly on Open Days, is a two-storey foyer to the hall and contains a stairway. The hall itself and the stage are elevated on stilts and the hall is designed as an auditorium. Beneath the hall

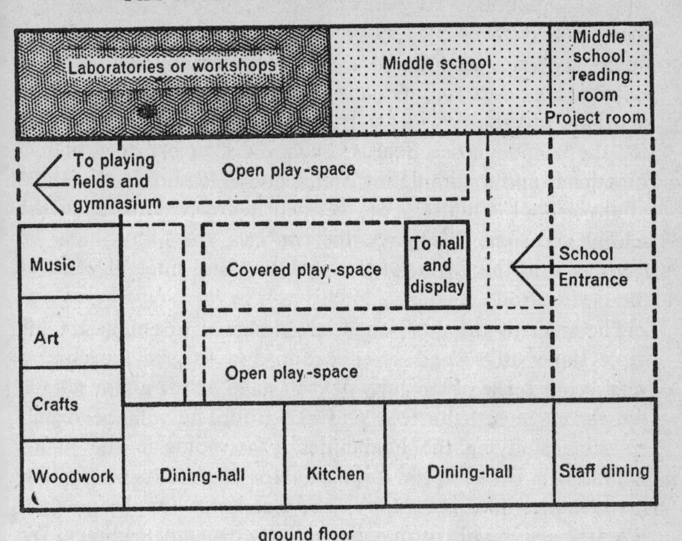

Diagram 9a *A Plan for the Secondary School* (*ground floor*).

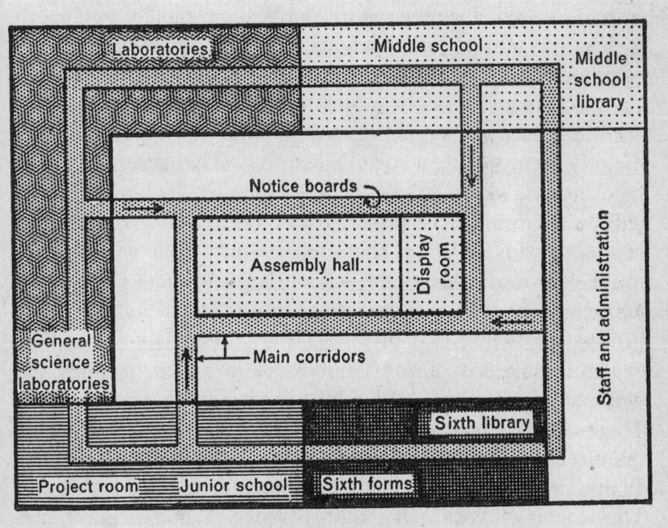

Diagram 9b *A Plan for the Secondary School* (*first floor*).

there is a covered play-space which is complemented by an open play-space on either side. On all sides of the hall there are elevated corridors for circulation between first-floor classrooms and laboratories. A wider corridor on one side provides space for the school notice boards. Such a design provides both a functional and a stimulating architectural feature in the midst of the school. Children, we feel, will learn to look upon the school occasions, the plays, the concerts, the film-shows, the lectures, and the Open Days as exciting and integral parts of their education.

The sides of the quadrangle are designed to emphasize the three stages of secondary education and to give the child a very strong sense of the unity of each stage. In the junior school, the eleven plus to thirteen plus age-group, he will spend half his time studying the humanities. Classrooms in the junior school will be equipped primarily for the study of English, mathematics, and geography. The classroom for the younger boy will also be his form-room with its own small library. We do not consider that the junior school needs a library of its own. Adjoining the classrooms we site the project-room, which will be the hub of junior-school activity both during and out of school hours. A staircase will lead directly from the project-room to the ground-floor rooms for woodwork, crafts, pottery, art, and music. The junior school will use the dining-hall directly beneath their own classroms. The general science laboratories, which will be the ones used by the junior school, will be adjacent to the project-room. With such a grouping of rooms we do not think that the younger child will need to move very much during the school day, and there is an excellent chance that he will regard the junior school as very much his own particular part of the school.

The middle school and laboratories are sited together and will occupy about half the total teaching space of the school. There will be a great deal more mobility in the middle school than in either the junior school or the sixth forms. Classrooms at this stage must be specially equipped for their own subjects. The teaching of English requires plenty of books, plays, and reference material; these must include sets of books which can be used on loan to the class. There must also be a record player for listening to poetry or readings from Shakespeare. Access to a tape recorder is another essential, for a child will not speak well until he has first discovered just how blurred and indistinct his native speech is. Modern language rooms need these basic aids to speech training. They also need display panels for showing something of the culture of the country; more shelves for reference books, and space for the display of pictures, photographs, and posters. A good modern language room should in fact exude, as far as can be done on foreign soil, the atmosphere of the country. Mathematics rooms must have a large amount of blackboard space as well as facilities for using demonstration models. The children must have flat-topped desks for their work. Geography and history rooms will need bookshelves for much illustrative and reference material as well as roller-type maps and wall-charts. Screen and projector, and if possible epidiascope, are essential to these rooms.

In the middle school the children will circulate and each classroom will be the domain of a particular teacher. In the middle school the concentrated study of science will begin and therefore the laboratories are sited so as to avoid waste of time between classroom and laboratory.

Children of this age, thirteen plus to fifteen or sixteen plus, will spend much of their spare time in physical activity. Therefore the approach to the playing fields and gymnasium is adjacent to the middle school. But at the other end of the building, in a quiet corner, there is the middle-school library, and on the ground floor the reading-room and project-room. Very often middle-school libraries are a poor shadow of sixth-form libraries, and in consequence many children have lost their taste for reading before they even leave school. The middle-school library, we consider, should be as well stocked as any other school library, and under the care of an experienced member of the English teaching staff. It will be run under normal library rules regarding behaviour and the borrowing of books. On the other hand, the reading-room and project-room on the ground floor will be a place where children can relax and pursue their own hobbies – under adequate supervision. Finally, as the middle school usually contains the rowdier members of the community, we have sited it nearest to the rooms of the head and deputy-head!

The sixth-form classrooms are located next to the junior school, and like the junior school they will form very much of a unit on their own. Each sixth form will have its own room in which the formal classroom will give place to table and chairs. The sixth-form library will adjoin the sixth-form classrooms. Not only will this library provide all the specialist material for the sixth forms, it will also be large enough and convenient enough for teaching combined sixth forms when they come together to study, for instance, 'The Development of Scientific Thought'. This sixth-form library will substantially replace what in many schools is now the school library. We do not consider there is any case for having a specifically 'school' library. All too often such a library, standing on its own in a part of the building not close to any particular section of the school, serves a limited purpose, and sometimes even remains largely unused by the sixth-formers whom it is designed to serve. By placing a library adjacent to the sixth-form classrooms there is a good chance that sixth-formers will use it all the time, and that a pre-undergraduate approach to literature may develop amongst older children. The fact that sixth-formers are the farthest away from the laboratories is of no consequence. Unlike children in the middle school, who may spend not more than a double period at any one time on science, the sixth-former will frequently spend a whole morning or afternoon in the laboratories. He will have plenty of time for moving to and fro.

The administrative offices adjoin the entrance to the school. These will comprise rooms for the head, deputy-head, bursar, and secretaries. It is also important to site the staff-room and dining-room here. A well-equipped and comfortable staff-room is not a luxury but a necessity. Very often in the past this has not been so. 'The defects from the staff point of view of many old schools would never be tolerated in office or factory.' (27) Let us get rid once and for all of the notion that teachers, just because they are teachers, will put up with inferior working conditions. One of the additional reasons why there is a good deal of space for administrative offices is that more secretarial help will have to be made available to the teaching staff in schools in future. At the other end of the building a broad way leads out to the playing-fields and gymnasium. If we had any money it would also lead to the swimming-bath.

Externally such a school would look not unlike that designed in 1953 by Denis Clarke-Hall at Cranford in Middlesex. Also, it has close affinities with the school at Hunstanton designed by Alison and Peter Smithson. The external view would perhaps not have the grace of the forecourt of Eton College. On the other hand, it would, we think, offend the young eye much less than the great functional blocks which so often make the modern school indistinguishable from an office block or a factory building. Some simple landscaping, even the planting of a few trees and the plotting of gardens, would greatly help to humanize the external outline of the building.

Within the quadrangle this design would promote the aim of educating a community of children. From the beginning the child would be learning that knowledge cannot be compartmentalized and that classroom work is always complemented by what is learnt in assembly, laboratory, library, and workshop. At the same time, he would experience the comradeship of his own age-group and its setting in the wider community of the school as a whole. Over and above these insights, we consider that by going to such a school the child would absorb that intangible quality of atmosphere; that he would find life in such buildings both challenging and stimulating.

A static design will not do. The number of children of school age for whom the local education authority must cater in any given year cannot, we fear, be predicted with mathematical accuracy. But a school once built must serve the community for many years. Therefore, there must be some slack space in a new school. Two or three classrooms should be incorporated in the school over and above the number required at the time when the school is built. Plans should also be made for expanding the existing buildings without interfering with the design of the school and its character. Building funds, like the children, are unpredictable. A new school should allocate space for buildings, a swimming-bath for instance, which it may not be economical to construct when the rest of the school is being built. In this way we can have a flexible plan for the future.

Houses are built to bring up families. Factories are built to make a certain product. Hospitals are built to cure the sick and suffering. Schools must be built to educate children. In this chapter we have drawn attention to the fact that schools are not often designed with this aim in view, although the buildings may exhibit other admirable qualities. The plan which we submit is diagrammatic, but it contains an idea capable of modification to the particular site on which the school has to be built. It is a plan which would enable the kind of secondary education we have advocated to take place.

CHAPTER 12

Educating the Intelligent

INVESTMENT in people is the theme of this book. Each individual man and woman is of unique value, and we believe that the political, economic, and social policies of Britain must be judged by whether they enable men and women to develop their individuality. At this stage in our affairs our investment must be directed towards the most intelligent forty per cent of Britain's children, most of the first and second quartiles of the Crowther Report. These children are the first priority for the future. They are the greatest vein of untapped talent in this country. Today we invest inadequately in all but a minority of them and even this minority receive an education that is ill-adapted to the second half of the twentieth century. The reason for directing our investment towards these children, who are themselves a minority of the total number of children, is that where they lead others will follow. If we can give the best possible education to forty per cent of our boys and girls the problem of educating the other sixty per cent should be immeasurably easier. The forty per cent with whom this book is concerned are all those children who are capable of taking the Certificate of Secondary Education or any higher examination.

Educating these children is the problem of educating the first generation. Their children, the second generation, will join the ranks of the enlightened – if our experiment has been successful – and will passionately want to educate the third generation. Our problem is with the first generation. We are in the position of the sales manager launching a new product on the market. We have got to persuade large numbers of intelligent children, whose own parents were educated in overcrowded elementary schools which they left at the age of fourteen, that education is fun. For the first generation it is a straight fight between the school and the attractions of the great world. We must persuade them that school is not a bore; that school competes. They *can* receive an education that is something just external to their lives, an education that makes no contact with the things that they really want to do or the kind of people they really want to be. Such an education is a waste of time and money. Or they *can* take part in an education that strives throughout to meet them on their own ground, guide them towards realizing their own ideas, and relate their own personalities to the world they are living in. Which is it to be?

The right curriculum is the only way to convince children that they are not wasting their time at school. The major part of this book is about the curriculum. An attempt has been made to answer the question – 'What does a child need to learn at school?' The needs have been reduced to those which are essential from the point of view of the child himself and from the point of view of society. The new curriculum has been designed to meet these needs throughout a child's secondary education. It has been designed at every stage with the existing curriculum in mind in order to facilitate the changes which are suggested. The new curriculum could be introduced into schools if enough of us wished it to happen. It could be introduced experimentally and modified by different schools and different teachers during the next decade. It is, furthermore, a curriculum that is designed to educate children in such a way that they will gain an idea of the unity of knowledge. Above all it has been designed to show them that their education is absolutely relevant to life itself. It is a curriculum that can challenge them, excite them, and answer their deepest needs.

The right curriculum must be presented to them within the framework of the right school. Children are looking for a moral answer to the enigma of life. Schools cannot suggest a moral answer that is very different from the answer that the children will get from their homes and from their society. But people expect schools to do just a little bit better than they normally do themselves. School is the child's society during the years when he is growing up. It is his first society and it is the society which will have the most influence upon him. Only his home can form stronger ties than his school, and they are ties of a different nature. Therefore we must do all that we can to make the experience of school one of the most fascinating experiences of his life. The moral answer that the school should give is the conviction that *together* human beings can achieve something that is greater than the sum of all the parts.

The right curriculum within the right school and taught by the right teachers. The arguments put forward in this book in favour of higher salaries and better training for teachers are a reasoned assessment of how we might move towards a teaching profession capable of undertaking this great task. Investing in teachers is, once again, investing in people. Unlike the installation of a new piece of factory machinery the payment and training of a teacher cannot be calculated in financial terms of capital outlay, working life, and replacement cost. Bad teachers will give us almost no return on our investment; good teachers will give us a return beside which the most productive piece of machinery will appear paltry and inadequate. But if you want to produce goods of high quality you do not pare down your expenditure on machinery. This book contends that curriculum and school are a mere façade if they are without intelligent, enthusiastic, and persevering teachers.

This book is addressed to the British public whose children the schools hold in trust during the critical years of adolescence. It is addressed to the parents whose deepest wish is that their children should grow up to become a little better, a little happier, a little more perceptive than they have been themselves; to the parents who have invested in the future. It is addressed to the industrialists who believe that the factories, the farms, and the shipyards should maintain and increase the wealth of this nation and should use this wealth in the long-term interests of society rather than for immediate gain; to the industrialists who have invested in the future. It is addressed to English men and women who pay taxes and who care what kind of country they live in and whether it is a country moving towards greater freedom and a more civilized way of life; to our fellow countrymen who have invested in the future. This book has been written because the authors believe that all these people would say that their plans for the future depend upon 'Educating the Intelligent'.

REFERENCES

1 A. G. Bartlett, an article in *The Times Educational Supplement*, January 1961.

2 Isaiah Berlin, *Karl Marx*, second edition, Oxford University Press, 1948.

3 Board of Education, *The Teaching of English in England*, H.M.S.O., London, 1921.

4 A Bow Group Memorandum on Salaries of Teachers in Primary and Secondary Schools, Bow Group Publications, London, 1959.

5 A Bow Group Pamphlet, *Patronage and the Arts*, Bow Group Publications, London, 1959.

6 A Bow Group Pamphlet, *Willingly to School*, Bow Group Publications, London, 1959.

7 J. L. Brereton, *The Case for Examinations*, Cambridge University Press, 1944.

8 A. Buchanan, *The Film in Education*, Phoenix House, London, 1951.

9 E. B. Castle, *Ancient Education and Today*, Penguin Books, Harmondsworth, 1961.

10 Cyril Connolly, *Enemies of Promise*, revised edition, Routledge & Kegan Paul, London, 1949; Penguin Books, Harmondsworth, 1961.

11 W. B. Curry, *Education for Sanity*, Heinemann, London, 1947.

12 J. Dewey, *Democracy and Education*, The Macmillan Company, New York, 1961.

13 *Directory of Opportunities for School Leavers*, Cornmarket Press, London, 1960.

14 The Duke of Edinburgh's Award: Pilot Scheme.

15 *Educational Research*, June 1960.

16 *Ençounter*, December 1958.

17 W. D. Evans, General Studies Research Group, 1960.

18 *Evening Standard*, May 1961.

19 H. J. Eysenck, *Sense and Nonsense in Psychology*, Penguin Books, Harmondsworth, 1957.

20 *Guardian*, January 1961.
21 *Guardian*, January 1961.
22 *Guardian*, January 1961.
23 *Guardian*, August 1961.
24 G. A. Highet, *The Art of Teaching*, Methuen, London, 1951.
25 Harvard University, *General Education in a Free Society*, 1945.
26 Lord James, *Education and Democratic Leadership*, 1961.
27 Peggy Jay, *Better Schools Now!*, Turnstile Press, London, 1953.
28 *Journal of Education*, January 1953.
29 *Journal of Education*, March 1953.
30 King George's Jubilee Trust Report, *Citizens of Tomorrow*, Odhams, London, 1956.
31 *Listener*, September 1959.
32 *Listener*, June 1960.
33 Sir Philip Morris, *Pioneers of English Education*, Faber & Faber, 1952.
34 W. R. Niblett, *Christian Education in a Secular Society*, Oxford University Press, 1960.
35 Stanley Nisbet, *Purpose in the Curriculum*, University of London Press, 1957.
36 *Observer*, December 1958.
37 *Observer*, January 1961.
38 Oxford University Department of Education, *Arts and Science Sides in the Sixth Form*, 1960.
39 Oxford University Department of Education – Conference 1961.
40 A. D. C. Peterson, *Educating Our Rulers*, Duckworth, London, 1957.
41 Political and Economic Planning – *Parents' Views on Education*, 1961.
42 *Physical Education in the Primary School*, Part 1, Ministry of Education: H.M.S.O., London, 1957.
43 Lord Radcliffe, *The Problem of Power*, Secker & Warburg, London, 1952.
44 Report of the Central Advisory Council for Education, England, *Fifteen to Eighteen* (the Crowther Report), H.M.S.O., London, 1959.
45 Report: *The General Certificate of Education and Sixth-Form Studies* (the Lockwood Committee Report), H.M.S.O., London, 1961.

46 Report: *Secondary Education with Special Reference to Grammar Schools and Technical High Schools* (the Spens Report), H.M.S.O., London, 1938.
47 Report: *Secondary School Examinations Other Than G.C.E.* (the Beloe Committee Report), H.M.S.O., London, 1960.
48 J. M. Richards, *An Introduction to Modern Architecture*, revised edition, Penguin Books, Harmondsworth, 1956.
49 Ronald Rubinstein, *John Citizen and the Law*, Penguin Books, Harmondsworth, 1947.
50 Science Masters' Association and Association of Women Science Teachers' policy statement, *Science and Education*, 1961.
51 J. H. Simpson, *Schoolmaster's Harvest*, Faber & Faber, London, 1954.
52 W. O. Lester Smith, *Education*, Penguin Books, Harmondsworth, 1957.
53 C. P. Snow, *The Two Cultures and the Scientific Revolution*, Cambridge University Press, 1959.
54 Herbert Spencer, *Essays on Education*, Everyman's Library, Dent, London, 1906.
55 *Sunday Times*, February 1961.
56 *The Teaching of Mathematics in Secondary Schools*, H.M.S.O., London, 1958.
57 Thirty-eighth Yearbook, National Society for the Study of Education: *The Development of Ability in Arithmetic*, 1939.
58 *The Times*, January 1961.
59 *The Times*, letter to, June 1961.
60 *The Times Educational Supplement*.
61 *The Times Educational Supplement*, July 1958.
62 *The Times Educational Supplement*, September 1959.
63 *The Times Educational Supplement*, February 1960.
64 *The Times Educational Supplement*, February 1960.
65 *The Times Educational Supplement*, June 1960.
66 *The Times Educational Supplement*, October 1961.
67 *The Times Educational Supplement*, March 1961.
68 Asher Tropp, *The School Teachers*, Heinemann, London, 1957.
69 A. J. Toynbee, *Civilization on Trial*, Oxford University Press, 1946.
70 *Universities and Left Review*, Autumn 1958.
71 J. Vaizey, *London and Cambridge Bulletin*, No. 35, 1960.
72 J. Vaizey, *The Costs of Education*, Allen & Unwin, London, 1958.

73 V. Welton, *Burning Coals of Fire*, S.P.C.K., 1961.
74 A. N. Whitehead, *The Aims of Education*, new edition, Williams & Norgate, London, 1950.
75 Raymond Williams, *Culture and Society, 1780–1950*, Chatto & Windus, London, 1958; Penguin Books, Harmondsworth, 1961.
76 *The Younger Generation:* report of the Labour Party Youth Commission, 1959.

Index